THE SOUL STYLISTS

FORTY YEARS OF MODERNISM

PAOLO HEWITT

MAINSTREAM
PUBLISHING

EDINBURGH AND LONDON

First published in Great Britain in 2000 by
MAINSTREAM PUBLISHING COMPANY (EDINBURGH) LTD
7 Albany Street
Edinburgh EH1 3UG

Reprinted 2001

ISBN 1 84018 228 8

A catalogue record for this book is available from the British Library

Typeset in Battleaxe, Garamond and Gill Sans
Printed and bound in Great Britain by Butler and Tanner, Frome and London

Dedicated to the greatness of black music, black culture and the black race who have given so much to inspire us.

PAUL WELLER

Dedicated to all the Woking Suedeheads, whose style and attitude filled my mind with a million possibilities.

PAOLO HEWITT

There are so many people to thank for their part in this book's birth, but I particularly want to single out Val Wilmer and Kevin Johansen, whose generosity and help have been invaluable. I also want to thank Debbie Hicks for transcribing the tapes with her usual professionalism and brilliance. Many thanks. *P.H.*

Contents

'You never look backwards at that age.

     What for?

This is what's happening now.

     You need the music to go with the lifestyle

to go with the attitude.

     Forwards, no looking back.'

NORMAN JAY, DJ

FOREWORD

By paul weller

FLAKS WAS A PROPER *BOUTIQUE*, the very first in Woking. It had a blacked-out front window save for a centre circle of clear glass which gave the effect of peering into Aladdin's cave.

I'd been in there a couple of times just to gaze in wonder at the explosion of colours and styles that the late '60s had to offer a clothes and music-obsessed twelve-year-old. At that time, all I craved was a tie-dyed grandpa vest and crushed-velvet flares.

But '69 turned into '70 and in a small suburban town things slowly, but very noticeably, changed. On a day that I will never forget, I saw a kid I knew from school wearing a pair of jeans which were the most fantastic shade of blue I'd ever seen and these I gradually learnt were Levi's. (I was still in Tesco Bombers.) More and more, I started noticing a lot more kids at school because with these blue jeans, many of them now added a red and white gingham button-down shirt. It was a look I had never seen before. It caught my imagination. And never let it go.

The more I noticed the new shift in everything the more intrigued I became. I'd saved up the money needed for my first petrol blue and red-checked short-sleeved Brutus shirt, eventually adding the Levi's which I got from the local Co-op, priced 50 shillings (£2.50). These were the jeans that were shrunk to fit by sitting in a cold bath. I'd just missed out on blue shiny 'wind cheaters' with red, white and blue cotton collar and cuffs, which mates called monkey jackets. But I did catch: DMs, loafers, plain or with tassels or even more beautiful – tongue and tassel, Royals brogues or smooths, Levi Sta-prest trousers in black, pure white, off white, dark blue, petrol blue, ice blue, bottle green, light green, Harrington jackets in all shades, Crombie coats, Prince of Wales checked pants.

And so it went – the most fantastic clothes I had ever seen. A lot of the time you'd see the older brothers, sixteen-plus, who to us 'peanuts' were real faces, off out for a night in a Tonik suit jacket, red Fred Perry, off white Sta-prest or faded Levi's, red socks and Oxblood smooths or black Royals. For me, that look was just incredible. It's an image that always comes back to me as the true mark of style. It was so exact, so precise, so neat, streamlined, clean, hard and totally expressive. Like all great fashions it came from the grass roots upwards, street fashions made for the kids by the kids involved. In lots of ways, it is the very heartbeat of this book.

The Soul Stylists is a testament to a hidden post-war working-class culture, devised and made up as it went along, constantly changing and turning into something new and fresh. It was made by English working-class kids and was never swayed or influenced by the big fashion houses or the faceless money men. Rather, it remained totally autonomous and brilliantly creative.

It was also silently rebellious in lots of ways and outside of politics or mainstream culture. The look, attitude, music, the lifestyle was largely undetected to society until the media latched on. And then it was only to highlight – as usual – the negative sides (violence, drugs, etc.). But it's the positive, upward sides that are enduring and will continue to be for they can not kill off what they can't control.

Forget 'em because in my mind I'm back to the images of a Tonik suit that came in blue and red – or blue and orange, or smokey blue and green, or bronze and black – hearing 'Sex Machine' at Woking Football Club, or '54 – 46 (Was My Number)' at a fairground. Or going up Petticoat Lane for the first time. Girls in white holy-cow tights and two-piece Trevira suits and daydreaming about Julie Driscoll's hair and make-up and her influence on the Skinhead girl look.

By 1970 or '71, I didn't know anyone who wasn't a Suedehead. At the weekly dance I'd watch out for the couple of guys who would wear something you'd never seen before, but what you'd all be wearing in a month's time. The changes came quick and fast. By 1971, it was beige polo necks, checked Rupert pants, Budgie jackets and the hair longer and feathered out. And so we all moved on in different ways. I went the all-scruffy-in-a-rock-band look for a while, others stayed with it and went into army shirts and Oxford bags and the Sound of Philly.

It all made an everlasting impression on me. I took it very seriously and I always will because in a very cultural way it has been a huge influence on me. It helped me to find and think of different worlds, of different possibilities, of different ways that life can be. And it's in this sense that I feel it is a faith. A true one.

In this book Paolo has tried to speak to those at the dawn of each respective scene and tried to trace the branches that lead back to the same tree.

We hope we've got it right. We hope you dig it. What we do know for sure is that this book contains a history that is unclosed and forever moving on.

THE SOUL STYLISTS

PREFACE

THE DAY BEFORE YESTERDAY, I hit the smell of freshly cut grass and unexpectedly it sent me spinning backwards to that space in my mind when I was 12 and The Look swept through my school. Even now, I still don't know how it happened.

We had been nothing kids, dressing nowhere. Then one day, I still recall, I came into school and for a moment I didn't recognise any of my friends. As if on cue, all of them were dressed similarly, in Levi Sta-prest trousers and shoes which were either brogues or loafers with red socks. They sported Ben Sherman or tartan-checked Brutus shirts and they covered them with Harrington jackets or Crombie overcoats.

I was stunned. The Look was neat, functional and compelling to gaze at. But more than anything else, these clothes irrevocably changed my friends, turned them instantly into young adults. You couldn't look innocent in these clothes. They made you touch manhood. This Look, like the promise of those early days, never left me. What I didn't realise – and Paul Weller did – was that my friends were part of a continuum, a Mod tradition.

One sunny Marble Arch morning, when he was dodging the flak for applying strict Modernist principles and splitting up The Jam, Paul told me of The Soul Stylists. He showed how the Mod ideal had never died but had simply re-invented itself in different guises. In this book, we divide this unique layer of British social history into six British cults: Soho Jazzers,

Mods, Skinheads, Northern Soulers, Soulboys and Casuals. And although each scene is based on differing music and clothes, there is no doubt that the principles and attitudes of secrecy and exclusivity which underpin every one these movements have remained the same throughout.

Within this extended family, the most enduring and fertile relationship is the one that links British working-class fashion to contemporary American black music. Time and time again, this combination produces something unique and exciting. The first example of this process is to be found in Soho in 1948 when a small group of musicians emerged, calling themselves Modernists. In strict opposition to their counterparts, the Trads, these British Modernists dressed sharp. Their template was the style of their heroes – musicians such as Charlie Parker and Miles Davis, who were viewed as the finest practitioners of the new Be-Bop jazz that was emanating from America at the time.

Soul Stylism began with a British bid to emulate their wardrobes and lifestyle, which is why, in 1948, young musicians such as Ronnie Scott, Pete King, Dennis Rose and Tony Crombie created the Club 11. Soon, other underground jazz clubs had sprung up in its wake. All-night raves – and everything that entails – became the order of the day. Eddie Harvey, a Modernist who was there, tells me with a wink: 'Forget about the '60s. Soho in the '50s – that's where it was at.' But the arrival of rock'n'roll in 1956 stopped the Modernists dead in their tracks. Rock'n'roll was the complete antithesis of their lifestyle and its widespread success forced many of the Modernist movement's adherents to go underground and leave a space for their spiritual offspring to move into.

Their children were called the Mods and for them the secret of life was to be found in details: the length of the vent in your jacket; whether you should wear a vest or a T-shirt under your American button-down shirt; at what angle your pockets should be stitched. This is what mattered, this was where salvation lay, in having the best clothes, music and drugs. Mods built their world on this Holy Trinity. Music was their solute, drugs were their friends and clothes were their language, their means of expressing themselves to the world. It was a Soul Stylist principle that stretches up until today.

For Mods, quality was all. And that extended to their musical tastes which leaned towards the classic and enduring soul and jazz rather than passing fads. They, like their forefathers, openly embraced black culture – especially contemporary American soul, a music they did much to help establish in this country. But in 1963, the Mods' cover was blown by a TV music show called *Ready Steady Go*. The publicity which this show afforded the Mod movement diluted the essence of the scene. Many felt affronted that their way of life was being trivialised every Friday night. By 1964, the originals had joined their modernist elders in Ronnie Scott's and left so-called Mods fighting rockers on the beaches.

The next branch of the family was a direct consequence of the Mods' dilution by the media. The word skinhead is usually linked to violence and right-wing meetings. Yet the original movement was non-violent and non-racist and actually signalled a welcome return to original Mod principles of exclusivity. The basis of their whole look was American and derived from what is known as the Ivy League look – Ivy League being the collective name given to universities such as Yale and Harvard in North America. The main supplier of Ivy League clothes is the Brooks Brothers company, which invented the suit and the button-down-collar shirt.

This look became very popular in West London as a direct result of the Ivy Shop, opened in 1965 in Richmond, Surrey, by one John Simon and his partner Jeff Kwintner. Simon's aim was to dress young British executives in the same style as their American counterparts; but within a week their shop was filled with young working-class kids eagerly snapping up all their goods. What really set this new breed apart was their hair, which they shaved in the manner of American astronauts or marines. At the time it was an absolutely outrageous statement, so much so that some kids were sent home from school for wearing their hair too short.

As this style spread across London, different variations came into play. In the East End, for example, Dr Marten boots, Levi jeans, braces and Crombie coats became all the rage. But if there were differing stylistic variations, one thing united everyone: reggae music. Skinheads loved

THE SOUL STYLISTS

reggae. Furthermore, a lot of this new fashion had direct roots in the Caribbean world. The second generation of Caribbeans in London wore many items – braces, pork-pie hats and Crombie coats – which were then appropriated by their white counterparts.

It was, contrary to the public image that haunts skinheads to this day, the first sign of a society heading towards a healthy multi-culturalism. Skinheads became a nationwide phenomenon when, to the horror and disgust of the originators, the *Daily Mirror* used the word in an article entitled 'No One Likes Johnny'. Again, the publicity only served to hasten the purity of the scene.

Meanwhile, the growth of an offshoot from the Mod scene – Northern Soul – was gathering pace. Northern Soul devotees were basically Mods in the North of England who had created a scene based around obscure soul music. One of the first major clubs in the establishment of Northern Soul was the Twisted Wheel in Manchester, where a DJ by the name of Roger Eagle reigned supreme. Eagle played great black music, whether slow or fast blues, R&B, or soul music. However, the large-scale use of amphetamines at the Wheel's all-night sessions soon drove the crowd to demand faster music. Eagle quit in 1965 and the new DJs quickly bowed to the chewing-gummed and accordingly lifted the tempo.

The Wheel wasn't the only club to experience these demands. Many clubs north of the Capital experienced a similar process. Significantly, in 1973, the DJ Russ Winstanley opened up a club in Wigan called the Casino. At the time, it was like any other Northern Soul club. Fashion-wise, Winstanley's audience carried holdalls with changes of clothes in them that tended to be functional: vests, to keep you cool, and flared trousers because they looked good when you twirled. Musically, it promised to break new records and operated at a time when Northern Soul was a truly underground phenomenon . . . Until the fateful night when Russ Winstanley, against the wishes of his crowd, allowed a documentary crew into the club. The resulting programme attracted some 20 million viewers. Outsiders now rushed to Wigan, with the result that the original crowd moved out – and, once the thrill had died down, so did the outsiders.

In the South, soul was viewed in a different light. People in London wanted contemporary American black music and this music was called funk, metamorphosing later on into jazz-funk. It took years for the West End to create a space where a young, mixed audience could blend together; when it finally did, the club was named Crackers and was located in Dean Street. Here, a mixed clientele danced to edgy funk music such as Gil Scott Heron or the Fatback Band.

Outside London, it was the Goldmine, run by one Chris Hill, that made all the running. No one look dominated this scene, but a major fashion influence to emerge was the Soulboy's dress of mohair jumpers with leather trousers and plastic sandals. This was a look that later crossed over to the early punk clubs, one of the only times I can think of where soul has influenced rock music in this country to such a degree. When the original manager of the Goldmine left to run another club, the Lacy Lady in Ilford Hill followed. Six months later, punk happened and the whole thing ran out of steam. Its replacement was a cult, the Casuals, that developed completely unnoticed for several years and therefore eluded much photographic evidence. There are reasons for this paucity of documentary footage. The Casuals arrived at the same time as punk, a movement whose loud nature captured all the media's attention. It was also nurtured at football in a time when the game enjoyed none of its current popularity and was therefore not subject to mass scrutiny.

These two factors alone helped the Casual movement develop unhindered by media attention, and they account for the general lack of photographic evidence which brought us to formulate our decision not to use photos in this book. Although there has been some criticism of this policy, our reasoning was simple: if we couldn't get great shots of all the family then better to do without.

In this book there is much disagreement regarding the birthplace of the Casuals. One line I found interesting takes us again back to Jamaica, to a look pioneered by singers such as Gregory Isaacs. This style consisted of smart-casual tops (usually made by the likes of Gabicci), Farah trousers, white Bally shoes and plenty of jewellery. It was a look that became popular in Jamaica and then came to London sometime in the mid-'70s. The wearers of it were known as Sticksmen and were basically following in the footsteps laid down by the Rude Boys.

This style was first seen in places such as Peckham, a heavily populated Caribbean area of London, and then spread into such areas as Bermondsey and then onto the football terraces. Again, the persuasive influence of black fashion and music is evident and can never be underestimated. Outside London, similar fashion upheavals were taking place – for example in Liverpool, where a new look developed based around sports items such as Adidas trainers or tracksuit tops which were then mixed in with Lois corduroys or jeans. This initiated a craze to dress in expensive designer tops such as Ellese or Tacchini. As Liverpool were still a potent football force, they often qualified for European competitions. This allowed their fans to travel abroad and 'acquire' many of these sought-after clothes.

Musically, there was no one sound that defined the Casuals. Their fashion changes were dictated from the football terraces, not pop culture. No one band came to represent them, although this didn't stop the Casuals blending into the next phase of Soul Stylism, Britain's Acid House movement. We hope to tackle this development at some point in the future. Meanwhile, all I hope is that the people who created these scenes in the first place will not find anything in these pages that is wrong or that jars them. I hope we have managed to use their words and memories and attitude and paint their world in a convincing manner.

After all, it is the least that someone, given and taken so much by The Look, should attempt to do.

Paolo Hewitt
London
Spring 2001

CHAPTER ONE

THINGS TO COME

HIS HEAD IS FULL OF MUSIC. Crazy music. As he hastily walks his Soho street, his fingers dance against his thigh, picking out invisible notes on his invisible trombone. Melodies gush through his mind and musical scales hazily appear in front of his eyes. Music is a stubborn cloud that follows him everywhere. It may free him from the world but it chains itself to his spirit, so very reluctant to leave. Sometimes, he wishes that he was an accountant and his life was simple and he lived nine to five and then just when he starts imagining this easy life, damn you, back it comes again – the unshakeable strains of this crazy music.

A voice shouts out something – who knows what – and as he looks up, the invisible night wind drills straight into him. At last, a non-musical thought. He could kill for a Crombie. A three quarter length black number, made of the best wool, top pocket left-hand side and an inner lining made of silk. A Crombie tells a world recently robbed by war that you got cash, that against all odds you are making it.

* * *

Eddie Harvey doesn't have big cash. He is a musician. A trombone player and yes, he is on the up and up. But Eddie is still waiting, hanging on for that great moment in life when everything you want suddenly and

THE SOUL STYLISTS

magically appears before you and it all slots beautifully into place. Businessmen and successful dance band musicians wear Crombies. Poor musos don't, but that doesn't stop Eddie dreaming, daydreaming of the moment when he finishes off a 6 a.m. Soho basement session and then casually slips on his Crombie like it's the most natural thing ever – a second skin – and drawls, 'Want coffee?' to his jealous-eyed friends.

Understand now what a Crombie symbolises and what Eddie Harvey would give for one on this cold London night in 1948.

He moves briskly through the streets, heading for Bedford Square. He is Bloomsbury bound. Eddie wears a dark suit and it weighs a ton. Not surprising. It is made of barathea, a too-heavy wool material. He has on a white shirt and a black tie which has a block of sharp red running down half of it. Inside of him, in the pit of his stomach, determination mixes with excitement, protecting him from the curious looks he elicits from passers by, all of whom want to know one thing: why is that man wearing sunglasses at such a sunless hour? Carlo Krahmer knows why. He knows exactly why.

* * *

'Carlo Krahmer was a creature of the night. He really was. You only saw him after dark. Now he had some kind of contact in the States and he was importing records just after the war. Usually, they were aluminium discs. Amazing things. You see, during the war shellac was in short supply, they made those old 78s out of strategic material. They were using it for building aeroplanes, so they used to issue jazz records. One record a month, that's all you got. But that's all you needed. So we all used to learn this record and by the time we had had it for a week it had been played ten thousand times. You have to remember that the Musicians Union had banned Americans from playing here so unless you went to New York by playing on the liners going there you never saw these musicians.

It was actually quite funny. The American union was run by gangsters and the British Union was run by members of the Communist party and they never spoke to each other.'

Eddie Harvey – musician

* * *

Carlo is waiting for Eddie in his Bedford Square home – in his sitting room to be precise – and damn me if he isn't also wearing sunglasses. But they're for a purpose. Carlo is nearly blind. But he is never static. He is a drummer of big repute and also the proprietor of Esquire Records, his very own jazz record company. Carlo is a doer and a mover. He speaks in clipped tones and all his words are serious. They tumble out in a snappy fashion. Carlo never tells jokes. And he rarely smiles. But he fixes things, sometimes unintentionally. At the very first jazz festival in Nice, Carlo took over a young trumpeter called Humphrey Lyttelton. The French press got hold of Humph and casually asked him about his background. Humph, relaxing in the sun, went into one about his privileged background and time as a guardsman. Then he went off to play. Next thing you know the English press have gotten hold of the article and by the time Humph sets foot again in London, he's a massive star. Carlo, who set the whole thing up, didn't even flinch.

* * *

'If you liked that you should hear Charlie Parker.'

Art Pepper to British jazz musicians after
playing the 100 Club, Oxford Street

* * *

A lot of musicians – more than usual – are expected at Carlo's tonight. The word is out. Carlo has a new record from the States. What's more, it ain't any old tune. No sir. He's got the new Charlie Parker. From Soho, just the merest mention of Parker's name and its enough. They spread outwards, rushing towards Carlo's to hear this latest record, to buy copies and then learn it so hard and hear it so much that inevitably the music enters their bloodstream and then they can stand up in their small dingy Soho basements and play it without thinking.

They are Modernists.

They adore American music and hip jazz musicians. They dig American clothing. And that's why Eddie Harvey is wearing sunglasses after dark.

He is a Modernist.

* * *

'In the '40s, Charlie Parker and Dizzy Gillespie, they wore loose suits. That was the Professor Bop period. The original thing behind it was that they were trying to give jazz a scholarly feel because they wanted it to be counter culture to challenge the classical culture. It wasn't meant to be a popular culture, it was meant to be a new classical culture to depose the heavy-lidded opera and classical music types.'

John Simon – clothes stylist

* * *

For some, though, Eddie Harvey is not a Modernist. He is a traitor. He has sold out the cause, the trad cause. Traditional jazz music is the music of 1920s New Orleans, played by a number of British musicians. Even Eddie played it just as he plays a lot of other music, to pay the rent and smash the bills.

* * *

'I played in a big band. A lot of people did. It was the day of the big band.

We would go to Aberdeen and play to 2,000 people. I'm not kidding. The dance halls we played in were pleasure palaces. They really were. A lot of people were living in substandard housing and these dance halls were centrally heated and they were beautifully lit. They were just lovely places to go to and a great place to cop off. That always happened on the last number. That's when everyone made their move. They were rough places as well. I saw one guy pushed over a balcony and as far as I know he never got up again.'

Eddie Harvey

* * *

Eddie played trad. Then he saw the light because quite frankly, trad music does not ricochet around Eddie's head. No way. Trad is energetic, dancing music, frothy, happy go lucky and it appeals to guy and girl squares who wear duffle coats and baggy corduroy trousers. It is the absolute height of uncool. Mod is where it's at. You don't believe me? All you got to do is check out Johnny Dankworth. The man went on a boat bound for New York. He was a clarinet player. He landed in the Big Apple and then he heard Charlie Parker. He ditched the clarinet and came back an alto saxophone player. With a brand new wardrobe.

* * *

'Half of the trad lot looked like they had slept in their clothes but the modern jazz world wasn't like that at all. It was very smart. But trad jazz was very popular and got into the charts and so on. In fact, the author Jim Godbolt in his book, *A History of Jazz in Britain*, talks about trad as if it was an important event. Well, it was in that it was making money for people, but in terms of creativity, that was happening in the modern jazz world. Still, you can't ignore it because that was how the blues artists came over here. I was friendly with Chris Barber who played trombone and had

THE SOUL STYLISTS

one of the most successful trad bands; it was he who brought over Muddy Waters and Sonny Terry and Brownie McGhee and other people. That was very important in giving people the chance to hear that kind of music.'

Val Wilmer – writer

* * *

Prior to trad's success, the new jazz sound, typified by players such as Charlie Parker and Miles Davis, broke on the shores. They called it bebop and it turned jazz on its head. The music demanded that musicians burrow deep into their instruments, that they eschew every obvious musical move in search of new expressions they could find within themselves. It was a sound designed to keep out the great unhip and it was invented by black Americans who were making this music for reasons to do with race and class. To accompany this sonic assault on the straight world, a lifestyle, based around sharp dressing and night-time living, naturally evolved.

This life, with its insouciant manners and cool customs, was the life that Beat writers such as Jack Kerouac would eulogise and rhapsodise about. And this was the life that Eddie and Ronnie Scott, Pete King and Dennis Rose, Tony Crombie and all the rest of the Soho-based Modernists wanted so badly for themselves. Was there anything more glamorous than staying up all night, playing and digging jazz, getting a little high, maybe hooking up with a girl and making enough money to dress like heroes of the night? Since when was that asking for too much?

The Modernists based their lives around night time. Around midnight. They shunned the straight world with its fixation on time-keeping and obeying your betters and in doing so they became the first post-war whites – the first in a strong lineage that reaches us today – who openly embraced black culture.

* * *

'I got involved in jazz through a mutual school friend who was the cartoonist, Wally Fawkes. He turned me onto jazz and he picked it up because he was at art school and that's where the action was. Stylistically, I changed. I seem to remember tweed jackets, thick tweed ties, shirts with little tiny thin collars. That was the trad dress. I was in this band, George Webb's band, which was the first band to start the trad jazz revival. This music had not been played for twenty-five years. It was amazing that we got into it really because we had to learn it off records and there were so few of them. We learnt it all by ear. Then I had to go into the Air Force for a couple of years and when I came out the music had moved on. I heard this new music when I was in India. They had these forces radio stations and I remember the piece. It was "Things To Come" by Dizzy Gillespie. I thought the world had gone mad. It was such a big step from what I was used to.'

Eddie Harvey

* * *

Eddie had stepped out of the Air Force and into a London that was starting to wake up to many possibilities. It is tempting to believe that as war raged, London was a town filled with gloom and apprehension, that laughter never carried down its streets. Not so. During the war many people – admittedly, moneyed people – headed for West End clubs to dance and drink. There was a lot of marijuana smoke floating through the club air and a lot of bright young girls appearing through the haze, lively, energetic, on the ball, a delight to be with. War had broken down the barriers. These girls were not kitchen bound. They were sharper than that. They would not be like their mothers just as the sons would not dress like their fathers. For this fast set, help was always at hand.

Amphetamines were available from the Doc. Pills were diverted from their intended journey abroad to terrified UK soldiers and ended up in the surgery. Speed revved you up. It killed the fear that war had put inside your stomach.

So people took speed and they ignored the ravaged world because, put simply, that very night could be their last one on earth. Of course, in other less fortunate areas, the East End in particular, the temper of the people was noticeably sadder and angrier, envious even. And there are stories, true to this day, of musicians climbing through the East End debris and rubble and walking all the way into Soho to play at clubs such as the Cozy Hatch or the Fullado Club. So the London Eddie returned to was half alive, crippled but with a beating heart. That heart was Soho and its surrounding streets. It was a capital city that now contained a fair amount of black American servicemen. Ten thousand came to Britain in 1942. And in 1948, a number of these would join up with the new Caribbean settlers plus the Modernists and they would all congregate in Soho to create something lasting and worthwhile. From this mix, a new culture would slowly emerge.

These days, we call it soul stylism.

* * *

'With the musicians there was never ever any hint or even a mention of race or colour. No one even thought about it. You were musicians and that was it.'

Eddie Harvey

* * *

Sure thing, but not everyone was convinced.

* * *

'It was very difficult if a white woman walked down the street with a black man. Even in the 1960s, you would be stared at, you would be abused and sometimes you would be spat upon. One man insulted me at Waterloo

Station and I smacked him round the head and nearly got into a fight. I knew quite a lot of black men and that kind of thing was quite commonplace.'

Val Wilmer

* * *

For the cooler people, the jazz musicians, Archer Street, London W1 was the centre of the world. Here, on a Monday morning, they would arrive to pick up *Melody Maker* from the newsagent's stand, scour the ads and look to make contacts with those milling around. Those who could afford it tended to wear made-to-measure suits with square shoulders, lurid ties and Billy Eckstine shirts (designed by the jazz musician turned vocalist, the Eckstine shirt had a cutaway collar with a huge roll and was made and supplied by the famous shirt maker, Cy Devore). And every one of them tried catching the eye of one of the dancing girls in the nearby Windmill Theatre as they set about finding work for the week, the month or the year. Archer Street in 1948 was where the Modernists started laying foundations.

* * *

'Every Monday and Tuesday there were forty musicians down there, all talking about music and getting pissed and doing business. Nobody had phones in those days so you did business face to face. At that time there was a group of musicians who got together who were interested in this new music. Ronnie Scott and John Dankworth took this rehearsal room at the end of Windmill Street and they called it Club 11. It was the collective number of their groups. Johnny had a quintet, Ronnie a sextet.

'I got involved in this club and it was our university. There were guys down there who had great ears and they were figuring out all the harmonies and themes of this new music. Within months I became a different musician.'

Eddie Harvey

THE SOUL STYLISTS

29

Club 11 (and let's not forget Harry Morris on the door) started out as a rehearsal space for Modernists. But soon the bebop sounds coming up to the street started catching people's attention. Inevitably, the space quickly became a club. People would wander in at all times and check out what was going down. Later, it moved to Kingly Street where it was successfully raided for drugs. No matter.

There were plenty of similar clubs in Soho, dingy basement rooms that had been taken over by musicians and fans and hustlers, dark places where they would all cram in to play and hear the music. Outside, the Soho pavements were lined with people because television had yet to keep them in their homes. But the police were onto them now. They too had smelt the marijuana smoke in the air. They didn't like it. A war had been fought for order and for decency. So they shut the joints down. Not a problem. The promoters paid them lip-service and then opened up a new premises the next night. Girls and drink and drugs were around. It was plenty time. Eddie Harvey says, forget the '60s. The Soho '50s is where he is still at.

* * *

'The black influence was very strong because there were a lot of GIs and Caribbean people in the 1950s and 1960s and also a lot of Africans, which people always forget. Soho was very much an African place at one time.

There were quite a few of these black clubs around. They were dives but they were there in Soho just as they would be later on in Harrow Road and Ladbroke Grove.'

Val Wilmer

* * *

Of course, there were other established clubs. What is known as the 100 Club opened for business in 1942 when Robert Feldman took over the

THE SOUL STYLISTS

premises. Some nights, he and his two brothers entertained the crowd. That would be Robert on clarinet, Monty Feldman on accordion and 8-year-old Victor Feldman on drums (child star Feldman graduated to piano, played with Miles Davis, Cannonball Adderley amongst others, which is enough for any CV). The musical policy was to keep up to date but Humphrey Lyttelton started a trad night there in 1950 and the Modernists shut their eyes and ears to him.

* * *

'The trad world was very much a mix of art school and bohemianism. People would say, "I am a Bohemian" naming it as a style. My friend Janet that I grew up with, she went to art college and so she wore a duffle coat, black woollen stockings, heavy sweaters. In the trad world, the art school fashion was the dominant ideal although the majority of ordinary people, truth be told, were very drab. There were lots of trad bands originally put together by people who came into it because they liked the idea of New Orleans purism; this is working men's music, that kind of attitude. Of course, when Acker Bilk took off and made money from playing this, then suddenly everyone became a trad musician.'

Val Wilmer

'I think that what belies it a little is that all the photographs of the time are monochromatic, they're in black and white. But life was not really monochromatic, it was very colourful.'

John Simon

* * *

Club life provided two factions; trad versus Mod. First, the trads took over the Club 11 premises when it moved to 50 Carnaby Street. The new owner was clarinettist Cy Laurie and so was the club's name. Then in August 1952,

Jeff Kruger, a jazz-loving film salesman assuaged his nagging thought – why is every jazz club I go to always such a dive? – with the perfect answer when he ate dinner one night at the Mapleton Hotel near Leicester Square. He got friendly with the manager and was shown a basement, perfect for his needs. In August of 1952, the Modernists came to 'Jazz At The Mapleton' to hear the Johnny Dankworth Seven and Kenny Graham's Afro-Cubists.

* * *

'It was mainly full of burglars and whores. Fantastic people. They treated all musicians as if they were kings and queens. Also another place was the Blue Room which was one of Jeff Kruger's and the Café Anglais, they were all around Leicester Square.'

Eddie Harvey

* * *

A few months later, in honour of Graham's composition 'Flamingo', the club changed its name and began a succession of moves around town before settling down at 33–37 Wardour Street. Meanwhile, musicians such as Ronnie Scott, Tubby Hayes and Joe Harriott, through their music and dress sense, were becoming the leaders of the Modernist movement. So too were the likes of Johnny Dankworth, Jimmy Deuchar and Cleo Laine. And maybe a hundred others. These musicians, and the clubs they played in, attracted a diverse set of people with roots from all around the world. Music fans to the last, and looking to live outside the norm, the clubs were mixed, no violence, nobody being hurled over a balcony. In fact, they were havens from a country becoming increasingly hostile to the sight of non-white people taking to their streets. Jazz didn't care. Jazz thought otherwise. Jazz brought people together, to mingle, shake hands and hips.

* * *

'For me, I think it came to life in 1954. A lot of the Modernists used to go to the Lyceum. There was afternoon dancing there almost every day. Bands like the Don Lang Seven or Oscar Rabin. A lot of the kids who worked in offices used to go there lunchtimes. I was fifteen and my uncle made me a suit so I could go down there. It was a double-breasted grey flannel with an unusual shaped lapel. I still remember it distinctly to this day.'

John Simon

* * *

Stylistically, the Americans were still in charge. The Caribbean people in Britain, many of whom would have preferred to have headed Stateside but were prevented from doing so by the quota system established by the McGann and Walter Act, were to make a huge impact on British cultural life. But in terms of fashion – apart from the pork-pie hat – their initial impact was minuscule. The reason is simple. Like their British counterparts, they adored all things American. Inevitable really when you measure the distance between Jamaica and America. Just a twist of the radio dial in Kingston and you were picking up New Orleans. Which is why they were as hip as the Modernists when they arrived in England.

* * *

'There was a large Jamaican community in Harlem from the start of the twentieth century and a lot of them would send clothes back to people so that they would get all the latest modern clothing. I think the Jamaicans when they got here turned their noses up against outlets like Burtons who were off the peg and went to their own tailors. A lot of black tailors were also making suits at home on a freelance basis.'

Carol Tulloch – academic

THE SOUL STYLISTS

'In the late '50s, the American influence in Jamaica was almost total. Everything was copied. There was a colonial mentality. When I was interviewing people for my book, people kept saying, "You wouldn't accept something as really good unless it had come from abroad." You can't imagine what decades of colonialism and slavery before did for people.'

Lloyd Bradley – writer

* * *

The most identifiable part of the Jamaicans' dress was the 'windbreaker' trousers. They had straight legs which dramatically billowed out at the knee.

* * *

'That came about because the trousers they had, they got from the American rag companies. And they were hugely baggy so instead of tapering them all the way down the leg, they just tapered the bottoms and so you got that mad bulbous look.'

Carlo Manzi – costumier

* * *

This form of trouser soon disappeared from view to be replaced by a much tighter leg. That was because American musicians had now taken to wearing smart Brook Brothers clothes. Miles Davis was a prime example. Chet Baker was another. So was Stan Kenton. It was known as the Ivy League look, a title bestowed on the students from eight of America's major colleges – Brown, Columbia, Cornell, Dartmouth, Howard, Pennsylvania, Princeton and Yale. Its students bought their clothes from Brooks Brothers, a company associated with quality and a conservative look, which began trading as far back as 1818. In 1845, the company sold its first suit. It was a novelty, but not for the first time the company had broken new ground. Indeed, the company's reputation for quality clothing was sealed when Abraham Lincoln wore a Brooks Brothers coat on the occasion of his second induction into the American Presidency in 1864. At some point last century, the company settled on a classic design. Jackets would have two or three buttons (nothing more, nothing less) natural rounded shoulders and a back vent. The trousers would sit high on the hips but pleats were optional. The shirts would sport a soft roll collar which was buttoned down.

The button-down collar was their own invention. (It is said that company founder, John Brooks, attended a polo match and made note of the players who had fixed buttons to their collars to stop them flapping in their faces during the game. This could be a fanciful story. Doesn't matter. Fact is, Brooks Brothers gave the world the button-down shirt.) What is ironic about this look is that the American tailors who constructed the Ivy League appearance drew their inspiration from the upper-class British clothing of the time.

* * *

'The Americans tried to give an aristocratic look to everyone. It was an egalitarian culture. They wanted everyone to have equal opportunity. So in America, everybody wore Ivy League. I read in an American menswear magazine that 85 per cent of the business was in the Ivy League look. Huge money was turned over. They didn't have a tradition so in a sense it gave everyone a tradition. Ye Olde Ivy League look. The shield on the jacket pockets, everything referred to a subliminal tradition.'

John Simon

'In the early '50s a lot of guys wore that Ivy League look. Three-button jackets done up and short lapel on the top. Narrow trousers and they also wore flat-top haircuts. There was a famous jazz composition at the time called "Flat Top Flips His Lid". Now, before this Ivy League look everyone wore a suit. Even the guys digging up the roads wore suits. You'd see their jackets slung over a fence or something and they would be in suit trousers and a shirt digging away. Everyone wore a suit.'

Eddie Harvey

'The jazz culture was an Ivy League culture. Chet Baker and all those people wore Ivy League from the early '50s. They were your idols so you wanted to wear what they wore.'

John Simon

* * *

Along with the Ivy League look another major development in British menswear was taking place. Casual wear, rejected for years by the English male, was finally being accepted. It was a style that was automatically associated with Americans and, in Britain, resentment ran high against the USA. Their late entry into the war was hugely frowned upon. Wimps, sneered the Brits. And look at them now, dressing in loud colours, another word they spell all wrong. In the world outside of Soho it was considered totally unmasculine to be concerned with dress. Men – real men – wore their demob suits or they went out and bought dark conservative numbers. Colour was frowned upon. It was a sign of femininity. Suits remained rigid and so did their wearers. But Cecil Gee, a Lithuanian, was about to change all that.

Born in Vilnius, Lithuania in 1902, Cecil Gee came to London in 1914, just as the First World War was readying itself to take millions of lives. He was the middle child in a family of three, his father a fairly prosperous jeweller. Cecil was not obsessed with clothes, but after trying work in the family business he quit to find employment as a window dresser. From there, it was only a small step to borrowing money from his family and opening up his first premises on Commercial Road, Whitechapel in London's East End. The year was 1929.

'Most men in the 1930s were quite smart. Even if they were poor they were quite smart. It was important to be smart. The movies were the main inspiration because that was the main entertainment. It was where people went to hang out.'

John Simon

* * *

By the mid-'30s, Cecil Gee had moved to Charing Cross Road where he systematically took over the premises at numbers 106, 108 and 110 to create a three-floor menswear store. After the war he made a packet selling demob suits. Success suited him. It inspired him to greater things. One of his innovations was the sale of jackets and trousers on hanging rails. Another was the importation of American clothing such as Arrow shirts. Naturally, many Soho Modernists made their way to his shop. The name became hip.

* * *

'In 1959, a jazz package show came from America; Dizzy Gillespie, Dave Brubeck and Buck Clayton brought their groups and I got to know some of them. They played here and then they left to tour around the Continent. And then four of Buck Clayton's band came back to England and they specifically went up to Cecil Gee to buy their clothes. They were Americans buying British clothes. I remember I took a photograph of Dickie Wells the trombonist wearing an orange mohair sweater that he bought at Cecil Gee's. I used to look in the shop myself. The clothes were amazing.'

Val Wilmer

* * *

In 1955, Cecil Gee acquired more premises, this time on Shaftesbury Avenue. By now it was obvious that here was a bright man, a quick thinker, always looking to make the move that would excite customers. With the Gaggia coffee machine now available in London, Cecil set up a coffee bar corner for his customers. It was on the left as you walked into his shop. He also hung pictures of musicians on the shop walls. Cecil's imagination knew no boundaries. That's why he was not afraid to make trips to exotic places, like Italy, and learn from his European counterparts.

* * *

'I was a window dresser for Cecil Gee in the '50s. I remember he started off buying Scandinavian stuff first and then, in 1957, he went on a business trip with Ivan Topper who was a very well-known window dresser at the time. When they came back they brought some unusual stuff with them. It was Italian clothing, colourful jumpers, that kind of thing. I remember Ivan came into the shop wearing this amazing cotton suit, slightly Ivy League. That blew me away. From then on Cecil started importing stuff. He also brought a tailor back with him. His name was Giorgio. He was a fabulous tailor, absolutely fabulous. He made suits exactly like you saw in all those *film noir* movies.'

John Simon

* * *

With the British economy now starting to heat up, fashion could now take its natural course. Hence, some major competition. A competitor to Cecil Gee was Austins, found on Shaftesbury Avenue. It was opened by Lou Austin. A flash man, Lou. He didn't buy a house. He lived in the Savoy Hotel instead where he practised his saxophone. As befits a man with such tastes, his shop was full of American clothing and was the priciest in town. Then there was the expanding chain of Smith and Wesson shops.

And then there was Austin Reed on Regent Street, Cecil Gee's main competitor. The difference was that at Austin Reed you tended to push your face up against the window, look at the wonders displayed and sigh.

At Cecil Gee's you bought clothes. They were, unlike the man, affordable and stylish.

* * *

'He was not a stylish man. His clothes sense was very conventional but he was always immaculate. He was a dark suit and white shirt man, but he brought fashion into men's clothing. Austen Reed may have been first but they were never as influential as Cecil Gee.'

Gary Herman – Cecil Gee's nephew

'I remember he used to change his shirt twice a day. He was a very fastidious man.'

John Simon

* * *

Yet the Modernists had other things on their minds. America, they were discovering, was not only the country of Miles and Bird. It also created Bill Haley and rock'n'roll. For those who believed that the new jazz would inevitably become the new pop music, the world was about to give them a shock. They woke up one morning to find cinemas ripped to pieces by teenage hysterics and the papers screaming blue murder about Teddy Boys, rock'n'roll and leather jackets, knives, and some young American lewd called Elvis. Everything had changed.

* * *

'It was assumed or there was a sense that bebop music might become more popular than it eventually became. It never became really popular. It was too complicated. If you don't know anything about the music it is bloody confusing and that's one of the reasons why, when Bill Haley hit, rock'n'roll became very popular. The rhythm was so obvious that people could dance to it.'

Eddie Harvey

* * *

Young people who should have been enlisting in the Modernist cause now switched to American rock'n'roll. In 1956, Elvis's music invaded these shores. Teddy Boys (an Edwardian style that may have its roots in a look first pioneered by a group of ex-Guards officers) with their drape jackets and bootlaces, emerged. Cinemas became a gathering point. Marlon Brando starred in a film called *The Wild Ones* and the ton-up boys – leather jackets, jeans and motorbikes – duly appeared on the British landscape.

In Soho, the blues was now making a significant inroad into club culture. Alexis Korner took a residency at Studio 51 in Great Newport Street. Muddy Waters came and played in 1958 and confounded his adoring audience by using an electric guitar. (Dylan did the same thing eight years later but got far wider publicity.) Young Brits – starved of the music thanks to a non-existent radio service and unresponsive recording industry – began their own groups, attracting a young crowd for whom Bebop was not attractive enough.

Worryingly, for the Modernists, the '50s had also seen the rise of skiffle, a music pioneered by the likes of Lonnie Donegan and which was given breathing space at coffee bars such as the Two I's in Old Compton Street. Skiffle was related to trad and, for some observers, played an important factor in the development of blues and R&B outfits. It was frenetic music and it could be played easily. All you needed was a cheap acoustic guitar, a tea-chest bass and a washboard. This sound meant nothing to the Modernists who headed for the basements, waiting for someone like Ronnie Scott to finally open up a club on Gerrard Street – it would later move to Frith Street – and brave the storm.

* * *

'Ronnie's opened up in 1959. At first it was only a coffee bar with sandwiches. Then they got a licence for the bar. That was only open for a short time. Later on they had all-nighters there on a Saturday but there weren't any drinks. If people wanted to drink they would carry a half bottle or quarter bottle around. The laws were quite strict then. Of course, Ronnie Scott himself was one of the smartest dressed people around. The Marquee Club was on Oxford Street; there was a cinema called the Academy and it was under that. The back entrance was in Poland Street and all the musicians used to go in the Coach and Horses right there on the corner of Great Marlborough Street. The Marquee was open every night. You had Alexis Korner and his Blues Incorporated band with Cyril Davis on harmonica. Charlie Watts played drums, Jack Bruce played bass and there was also Dick Heckstall Smith on tenor sax and Graham Bond, who joined the band later.

Mick Jagger used to sit in with them and so it was all quite exciting. Then Joe Harriott and Tubby Hayes, they used to play there on a Saturday night and that was one of the big nights. Then the Marquee moved to Wardour Street but in the Oxford Street days the music was a mixture of many things.'

Val Wilmer

* * *

At the start of the '50s, Modernists thought they were going to take over the world. By the end of it they realised their dream was impossible. London was awash with clubs playing everything from blues to skiffle. Their music was just a stream flowing into a much bigger river. What they didn't realise was that it would be their spiritual sons and daughters who would take on the mission. It would be they who would go out looking like a million dollars and, with a brand new mind, they would spread the message all over this country.

* * *

'I was looking at a photograph of Clement Attlee wearing a suit and I thought, he's the prime minister and look at this suit and how badly cut it is. It really astounds you how badly cut suits were and that must be why, when John Stephens came through, he had to develop a new style of cutting, just like Vidal Sassoon with hair. At the time you didn't think anything of it, but when you look back you realise it was very different.'

Val Wilmer

CHAPTER TWO

The very tight circle

SUIT BY BILGORRI'S OF BISHOPSGATE and what a treat it is. Mohair, of course, with the jacket-front bearing two small lapels, three pockets and all with flaps, four buttons on the front, wear the top one undone. Jacket back we find two vents whilst your trouser creases are so sharp, cut you badly if you even dare glance at them in the mirror.

Shoes are basket weave from Raoul, shirt is Brooks Brothers, rolled collar and – nice touch – a Paisley cravat pushed inside that spacious collar. Hair is pristine cut, slight bouffant, sharp round the ears and forehead. Very European. And Americana. The job is in advertising. Office Boy. Not forever. You're modern, so is the work. One day you will be boss. You will be king. Capitalism is changing Britain fast. It's the time of the entrepreneur and failure is not an option. Defeat, unthinkable. Keep up sharp nose or you'll be picked off as easy factory fodder like the rest of your school links. Your daddy ain't rich and your mum definitely ain't good looking. The smog, the smoke and the war have seen to that. Now it's all for one and one is you. Very Americana.

Soon you will move into your own pad. Soho preferably. But you'll compromise within a 100-yard radius. Gotta stay West End because school and the family and the grimy two up and all the way down council terrace in Acton, all of it can go to the dogs along with your old man and his roll-ups and his gassy beer and belly. You've got higher things on your mind.

Drugs are amphetamines, the key to the promised land. Take three a day between the one liners and the put downs. Feel the voodoo rise inside, feel the head and soul fill with utter confidence, pure as water. You can move the mountain, defeat all enemies. You are Mod therefore you are invincible. You will go places your parents never even dreamed of.

Friday night is the Scene Club. Not inside the club, dick, but outside, in Ham Yard, where you pose and preen and deal in words, checking out the opposition. You were on *Ready Steady Go* recently. You wore your watch on the inside of your wrist. That night at The Scene, everyone copied. Now you don't wear a watch. What for? The weekend will end on Sunday night and that's a million years away.

You stand in the brisk night and sweet soul music floats on the air, an angel dancing into your soul. There's no other sound around that can match this. Tough beats, voices drenched in the meaning of sweat, driving horn riffs, those niggly guitars, the tambourines that beat upon the ground and those words, 'Ah hip-shaking mama, shake it to the east and shake it to the west'.

These records, they speak of a world where night time is the right time, daylight is for fools and the best clothes and records are made by the kings and queens of midnight. Aretha, I want to be there by your side but I can't and these are my young man blues.

John Lee Hooker passed through town recently. You had to laugh. All these smart white kids, fresh from their tailors and shops such as Alfs in Camden, gathering round him like kids at a birthday party, shouting for obscure B-sides that even he had trouble remembering.

These days you don't ask for the title of records when buying your tunes. You just march into the shop and name the catalogue number. 'Stax 600102' you say, or 'Atlantic 584256'. Modernists go to hidden record shops on hidden streets and grab imports for their own majestic service.

Sharp cookies. They cottoned on very early – unlike the ton up boys whose Brylcreem seems to have seeped into their brains – that black culture was just what the drab place needed so badly. Colour. Life.

Britain and the early '60s? Forget about it. It was the BBC in black and white and light entertainment and nothing on the radio and silly crooners and sexless singers and people fought to maintain this? Mods were radicals in silk, opening up their arms – welcome! – to all good things, wherever they came from, just so long as they opened up heads and changed the game forever.

At the club the Americans came and they sang their hearts out and the Mods nodded their heads and the girls danced and the DJ then kicked in with the latest R&B import and leather soles glided across the wooden floor, back and forth, twisting and turning. Four a.m. Cappuccinos in neon Soho follow, pills washed down with the caffeine, eyes wide open, brain ticking smartly until the shops finally dust themselves off and open up for another day and the Holy Grail begins, the endless quest for that immaculate jumper, that one shirt, that one item no one else has.

Home to change. Doris Troy and Wilson Pickett still rebounding around your head. Back out. Fresh face and fresh gear and something more for the upward direction again and please don't forget that come Monday you are going to tell that fat lard-ass of a boss where he can get off. And you will take his secretary – the one he drools over back in suburbia – out for a drink and a lot more.

As the London sun rises so do you, the best of Europe and America fused into one. No one knows for sure where you came from but no one will ever forget you, the first proper Moderniste, a real vision of style and a taster for the future. Modernism, the word came from the jazzers, the ones who shrieked in disgust at the trad sound the same as you did when you first heard the awful skiffle noise bouncing down Old Compton Street. The jazzers read the Beats, you check Albert Camus – both of you yearn for the freedom, both of you want so badly to pull back the country's curtains, let the air in.

Clothes, music, drugs, energy – they're all yours and as the pill dips for a minute, panic hits: soon you'll be too old for all this. Come that awful day which you can already see on the horizon, you had better make all your moves, ensured that everything you desire is in reach.

So you check yourself in the café window and melt into your reflection. You are ready again for the club, ready for the music, ready for the trip. It is your birthright. You are fifteen years old and nothing but the promise awaits you.

* * *

Famously, Mod came to the public's attention when *Town* magazine ran a six-spread on three 'faces' from Stoke Newington in London. They were Mark Feld, Peter Sugar and Michael Simmonds. 'The most important thing in the world to them,' ran one of the article's opening sentences, 'is their clothes; they have cupboards and shelves bulging with suits and shirts often designed by themselves in bright, strange and violent colours . . . the necessary ingredients are youth, a sharp eye for dressing, and a general lack of mercy towards the rest of the world.'

The year was 1962, a time when young cults, supported by music and fashion, could exist and breathe and take shape years before the media publicised them to a larger world and inevitably killed them. Which was Mod's fate. Certainly, there are some who say that when they read the *Town* article they thought to themselves, 'So there are others like us out there!'

* * *

'I think there are a lot of sources. I think the main source, ironically, is probably rationing, which extended beyond the Second World War and into the 1950s. You have to remember that's a rationing not just of things that we could buy in this country, but rationing due to the fact that there was a massive press on exports. So nothing that we were making that was any good was available here for many, many years. That goes for things like motorbikes, clothes, and all that sort of thing. And there were certainly no imports. And so what happened was, there was a very dreary twenty-year period after the Second World War, well, fifteen-year period. You have no idea how dreary it was. It was really dreary. And then what happened was that the first group of fifteen-year-olds born after the Second World War emerged into a world where they had some money to spend. And at the same time the British economy was being turned around. It was going from what's called a "command economy" to a "demand economy". This meant that things started to appear that people could buy and there were certainly imports starting to come in. Some of them were grey imports, things like Levi's coming through the PX Stores in American bases and moving into the black market via, you know, the East End markets and that sort of thing. So very slowly, and then quite rapidly, this purchasing power began to affect what was available. And this blossomed into a kind of early spring, if you like. I'm talking now around 1961, '62, and that's really when it started, although you can trace the movement, in terms of things like music and so on, back into the '50s with an interest in modern jazz and so on and those sorts of things. But popular Modernism began to emerge around 1961 and I think that's the real, the real sort of source of it, going back that far.'

Patrick Uden – head of Uden Associates

'When I started work, which was two weeks before my 16th birthday, I was always determined that I would have plenty of clothes to wear. I was always interested in looks as much as anything else. And I always loved black music. The first record I ever bought was The Impalas' "I Ran All The Way Home". It was on MGM over here. They were a mixed race doo-wop group and after that I think every record I bought – apart from Bobby Darin's "Dream Lover" – was a black record.'

David Cole – editor of soul magazine, *In The Basement*

'Another, crucial thing about Modernism is the fact that Britain is an island. That it's not get-at-able. I mean, if the government wish they can shut Britain off from the rest of the world. And in the 1940s and '50s that's pretty much what they did. The only influx of influence at all was from American bases which had been agreed on after the Second World War and the Americans brought with them everything that they had. So Chinos, Levi's, boots, shoes, trainers, golfing shirts, you know, all of that stuff, came with the Americans, including Coca-Cola of course which wasn't available either, believe it or not. There was also the fact that there were these exchanges that used to go on. I mean French girls would come and exchange with English boys and so on and so forth. So there was a little bit known, a little tiny bit known about the home cultures of these various countries. The whole idea that there was something out there was a sort of a pregnant period in Britain. And the Mods were the first generation to break out, to be reborn into a new world. To take from all of those things beyond the island and bring them back. And you have no idea of the impact in, say, 1954, of seeing a Lambretta with white wall tyres in London. I mean it was a complete shock. You couldn't believe it. Because everything else was an oily old BSA motorbike from before the war. And then suddenly there was this red and blue little machine with white wall tyres standing there. And it's a perfect product. And it's Italian. So you think, "Italy, this is a romantic place, there's things about Italy I want to know more about." British companies tried to make motor scooters of course and failed miserably, they couldn't do it.'

Patrick Uden

* * *

Shopping in the '50s in a Britain slowly recovering from the traumatic Second World War was not a joy. The goods that could be bought were mainly found in unfriendly department stores run and staffed by the middle-aged. There were no shops invented by the young and for the young. As for records, they were usually sold within large department stores. Often, you had to walk through the electrical department to get to them. There were, of course, exceptions.

'We used to go to Imhoffs which was a huge record store on Tottenham Court Road. You went downstairs and sorted out the records you wanted to hear. In those days I was absolutely bonkers about Ray Charles. I'd collect all the Ray Charles albums and then go into this booth with a record player in it and we'd smoke a spliff and sit in those booths all day. All those albums! We used to wear them out.'

Chris Hill – DJ

'Again, it's difficult for you to imagine what the world was like around 1960. But if you look at the Top 10 in that period you're talking about songs by groups that you will never have heard of called the Mudlarks, the Beverly Sisters, Helen Shapiro, you know. There was nothing, there was no "ch-bom, ch-bom" that you could dance to.

So the obvious candidate was Tamla Motown. These were the records, and records on the King label and that sort of thing. The music that came from Chicago, from Detroit, this was what you went for. And initially, again because of the restrictions on imports, these were usually produced as cover records in the UK. So you found that you couldn't get the original but you could get the cover.

But we didn't want the cover. What's the point of having a cover if you're a Mod? You want the original one. And if possible you want the original one on the original label. So immediately, of course, shops start to crop up all over the place and these guys used to go, literally, they would go to the States, they would buy records and they would bring them back and they would then sell them. That was their business. The one I remember best was the Charles Street Sound System but there were many others. So you went for Motown. You went for the Chicago Sound. Windy C, those sorts of labels. Little Anthony and the Imperials, that sort of thing. The Impressions. And this music didn't appear in the charts at the time. It wasn't chart music. It wasn't even Top 100 music. What happened was of course it slowly got released. It became available.'

Patrick Uden

'I used to subscribe to *Billboard* from the time I was fourteen. I used to look at all the charts. My father was quite friendly with the guy who ran the local record shop. All the record companies then used to bring out singles on a weekly basis and he'd have flyers as to what was coming out. He'd ask me what to order and I'd look at the *Billboard* charts and say, get me this or that. One day this guy in the record shop said to me, "There's another guy who comes in and buys almost exactly the same records that you do." So he introduced us. This guy was of Polish descent and it transpired that he liked the same tunes. He was two years older than me and he was coming up to London and going to a place called Transat Imports in Lisle Street.

You went in a little doorway and you walked downstairs to this guy and he had the most amazing stuff. It was nearly all black music. A lot of it had come through the States and this Polish guy said to me, "There's a lot more to Detroit than Motown." In those days, things spread very much word of mouth.'

David Cole

'At the time, you were either a Mod or a Rocker. There was no in-between.'

Phil Smee – designer

'Modernism was a uniquely English idea because it was born from the frustration of having nothing. To be a Modernist you had to come from a culture where Modernism didn't exist and therefore that made you different. And England at that time, Britain was ancient, it was falling to pieces. I mean it was awful. You have no idea, even by 1965, how miserable and grey Britain was. It was a ghastly place. I mean the first Habitat shop opened I think in 1962 in Chelsea and it was a complete revelation. Terence Conran, who himself, in a sense, is an early Mod, was a furniture designer, and he brought into Britain things that we had never, ever seen in England before and that Elizabeth David had described in her cookery books. And they were suddenly available in Habitat and they just walked out of the shops, you know.'

Patrick Uden

'It was considered cissy if a bloke paid any attention to his appearance. My father used to say very discouraging things to me if I was buying any clothes. I think it all started with the advent of commercial television and the way Burtons and John Colliers used to advertise themselves with this gimmick of the Saturday night suit. They would encourage males to dress up on a Saturday night. It was working-class culture because the people who dressed up on Saturday nights were the people who didn't have to wear a suit for work.

From that it probably became less of a strain for a bloke to look after his appearance. When I bought this PVC coat, which I got for 19/11d, my mother screamed down the road after me, "Don't come back to this house looking like that."'

David Cole

'The thing about being a Mod was that you had to be aware of very specific things. One of them was a rather east coast American waspish-ness. A sort of short haired, checked shirt, Levi's, desert boots, interest in jazz, interest in dancing. The sort of thing that appeared in *West Side Story* for the first time. And possibly before that in *Roman Holiday*, the famous Italian film. What happened in those films was they came from cultures where there had been success. In Italy there had been an economic miracle around 1949, 1950, largely a product of the Americans' intention of keeping the Communists out of power. They had poured money into Italy and Italian industry and subsequently they had been able to make many of the things that in Britain we never had. And you can list them. It's their motor scooters, their very sharp suits, it's their designer clothes, furniture, interior design, films, and so on and so forth. All of the things we didn't have here. So what was Modernism about? It was an acquisitiveness for the things not available in the UK. Hardly anything the Mods did was anything to do with the UK. Even the music was American music and then later Jamaican music because there was an off-shoot of Modernism which was West Indianism, put in simple terms. And there was a merging.

Many of the clubs were run by West Indians. West Indian music was played for half the evening and so on and so forth. So the acquisitiveness was for very specific things. It was not for anything. It was not just buying for the hell of it. Everything had to have a reason, a meaning, a double meaning, a deep meaning, and so on.'

Patrick Uden

'Radio Luxembourg was good in those days. The programmes were sponsored by record labels. In 1962, Oriole in Britain was the outlet for Motown Records and they used to sponsor a programme on Luxembourg two or three times a week.

You'd hear things like The Marvellettes, "Locking Up My Heart" and Mary Wells, "The One Who Really Loves You", that you wouldn't hear anywhere else.'

David Cole

'There was a very significant black influence and I say black because it wasn't just the West Indian influence, it was also the black American influence. The fashion influence that came through came from the style of the Tamla Motown stars, particularly in terms of mohair. The cut of the suit had nothing to do with it but the fabric did. The blacks here wore their trousers with a slightly tapered leg.

They wore their trousers shorter than we would wear them with socks showing. They tended to go for a tight fitting jacket and a squarer style. Fabrics were mohair and colours were a nice blue whereas we would go for stripes, diagonal stripes. Also, they brought in the idea of never doing your tie up. You always had a button undone. The influence was seen in the way they wore their clothes which was with a kind of arrogance that the Mods had as well.'

Ian R. Hebditch – original Mod

'We used to try and dress like the GIs. They used to give us white raincoats, the hats. It was like being in America. The West Indians, they wanted to be

Yankees as well so we would call them Bermuda Yankee or Jamaica Yankee. There used to be a little shop down the end of Shaftesbury Avenue – the Austins. We used to spend our wages in Austins. You could get the Bermuda jackets, the Ivy League look, the button down collars and all that. Charlie Watts was in there all the time. You'd always see him on a Friday or Saturday – whenever it was we got paid. We used to get our band uniforms in Austins because they had the American Ivy League look which was a forerunner of the Mod scene. My haircut at the time was the John F. Kennedy thing. And a lot of the GIs would have the razor partings. It was a great scene.'

Georgie Fame – musician

* * *

Unlike the teddy or ton-up Boys, with their outlandish style of dress, the Mods chose not to dress in opposition to society, they chose to infiltrate it instead. A well-dressed Mod was not a conspicuous creature. Like a chameleon, he blended in with his environment. His thrill was knowing that his adventures were illicit but his appearance was legal. The Mod always placed himself above suspicion. It was a completely new mindset to anything that had been seen before and its subtle approach would be passed on down the years.

* * *

'A lot of these boys went off and did jobs like bank clerks, and their managers thought they were fantastic. They'd never seen anything like it because you would be better dressed than your boss. I used to go to work and I was better dressed than my boss by a long way. It was a great way to be different and it also meant that if you ask me anything, anything at all, I'll know straight away if you're in the circle or not.'

Robert Hall – marketing director

THE SOUL STYLISTS

'The thing about Mods were, they were largely very Establishment. They looked the business. They were the first kids to have real jobs and they were proud of it, you know. They wanted to look like their fathers didn't look, so they wanted Italian suits, they wanted American shirts, they wanted Italian shoes, you know, they wanted American underwear. I'm wearing a Brooks Brothers shirt right now and you can tell at a thousand paces a Brooks Brothers shirt because of the roll on the collar. I know it's got a roll on the collar, I can tell that without even taking my eyes off you. Now any other Mod would know that. They would know an American shirt because of the double line of stitching around the sleeves. And an English shirt that was made to look like an American shirt, notably a Ben Sherman shirt, is not on. Okay.

Seven and sixers wore Ben Sherman shirts. Seven and six because they only spend 7/6d on their clothes. All that stuff. I mean it's a snobbery as much as anything else. But it was all to do with detail. It was all to do with detail.'

Patrick Uden

'I had a tailor – Murray Goldberg – who was a very good tailor but he couldn't understand what was going on. I told him once that I wanted a chalk stripe suit made and I drew how I wanted it. It had pockets which were angled out with a 45-degree flap and I wanted it hand stitched. He said it would ruin it. I said, no, I want hand stitching. Took me a hell of a long time to get him to do it. I said, "I'll take total responsibility but I want it done." He did it and then he called me and he was so excited on the 'phone. He said, "I've done it and it's fantastic." I remember going in there later on and he told me, "People are asking me for it now."'

Robert Hall

'You would admire something that somebody got but you wouldn't want to be like them. You'd want to go in your own direction because it was crucial that you had a good image. In fact, it was quite fundamental the image you presented. You had to keep changing it. You could not wear the same suit week in and week out. Obviously a leather coat was different but the rest of your clothes you varied.'

Ian R. Hebditch

* * *

Hard to imagine in our corporate now, but on every level of British society in the '60s, massive, fundamental changes were taking place. In music, in fashion, in cinema, in theatre, in literature, in politics, in public morality, on television and on radio, new ideas were taking a strong hold. British society, now buoyed by a healthy economy, not only made cash available but, it seemed, confidence as well. It was everywhere. In such a world the Modernist with his obsessive and crafty nature was inevitable.

* * *

'When I'm talking about a Brooks Brothers shirt and the roll on the collar and so on and so forth I'm talking about a London where there was only one shop where you could ever buy American shirts and even then they came in very small quantities. It was called Austin's, it was in Haymarket, no longer exists, and we would go up there and look at it. We would go up there and look in the windows, you know, and drool at these things, and penny loafers and things like that. So it was difficult to get. It wasn't easy. Very difficult to get.'

Patrick Uden

'All those shirts that came in from America, like the Van Heusen, they were all tailored shirts, they were tailored to fit in nicely inside slim trousers. There was no way you could have anything ballooning over the top. I really don't think you saw a fat Mod.'

David Cole

'Carnaby Street was a dreary sort of little alleyway when I used to go there. You didn't mind being seen there but as soon as it was mentioned in the papers, you never ever went there again in your life.'

Patrick Uden

'I went down to Carnaby Street and couldn't believe there were underpants in the window. It was so unusual to see underpants and they weren't the normal ones, they were quite tight, like briefs. This was in Adonis.'

Eugene Manzi – press officer, London Records

'You had to have briefs because the rise of the trousers were so low. You often only had a four-inch zip because it was such a low hipster. I remember the first time I went down there, a mate of mine said, "You guys want to go down Carnaby Street but watch it! It's full of poofs. It's where they all get their clothes."'

Carlo Manzi

'There used to be a place in Portobello Road called Lord Kitchener's Valet. I think they had another shop in Bayswater. They used to sell stuff that was the upper end of the market. You could also get better or different clothes in Lord John than you did in John Stephens. I also had suits made to measure in Burtons because even though they cut them from the template you could still have it as you wanted it. They might have a jacket with one vent and you'd say, no, I want two. And they'd do it. Obviously, they were cheaper than a tailor.'

David Cole

'I used to buy *Playboy* magazine. You know why? Because in *Playboy* you used to get fantastic pictures of Burlington socks. I got off on that because you didn't see pink or white Argyll socks here. There was no such thing. You'd see full length pics of men advertising clothes. They'd be wearing these great alpaca cardigans with baggy sleeves and trousers that were miles too short and that was the only male glamour that was available. See, you're talking to someone who thought that Austins on Shaftesbury Avenue was the best shop on the planet. If I met a girl I liked I couldn't wait to go shopping with her and show her how many shirts I could consume in an hour.'

Carlo Manzi

'If you talk to any original Mod he knows what smartness means. He knows what a gusset in a trouser is, or how a shirt should be made. I can look at a suit and know whether it's made properly or not. Just turn over the lapel and I know if it's a good suit. I don't need to see a label. You know things. How the suit should hang, the vents, the pleats, how many buttons, weight of material, how to press it properly. I used to press my suit with a wooden block. No one knows how to do that. Mod gave you an insight into what smartness was about – quality.'

Robert Hall

* * *

In high fashion, the work of designers such as Pierre Cardin and Hardy Amies was reflecting a huge shift in attitude towards menswear. In 1959, Amies had created a collection for the chain store, Hepworth's. He joked that the use of his name gave the suits he created, 'semi-couture status'. In reality, it was yet another example of high-quality goods being made affordable. Meanwhile, the French designer Cardin too was creating clothes of a distinctive nature. His collarless jackets when worn by The Beatles in 1962, for example, did much to take menswear to another level. Cardin also designed the clothes for the television series, *The Avengers*, taking John Steed's archetypal English wardrobe and fusing it with chic and continental touches.

Further abroad, in Rome, the tailor's school, the Academia dei Sartori was producing cloth craftsmen of an exceptional quality. Of those graduating, many sought work at Brioni, the tailors, also based in Italy's capital. They were attracted to such a prestigious firm because the name Brioni had become international. American stars – Sidney Poitier, Tony Bennett – flew in for fittings. So did Clark Gable and John Wayne.

Brioni's design speciality was a box-like jacket with narrow trousers, made from mohair or a similar material. It suited the Italian physique. In America, this Continental look – displayed by the stars – now squared up against the Ivy League. There was talk of who would take over but in the end – although both designs were updated – Brooks Brothers remained dominant. These shifts in the upper echelons of men's fashion quickly percolated down to street level. In Britain, men like Cecil Gee and later John Stephen adapted The Look and created even tighter designs for their young customers. In fact, the jacket in their hands became so short that it was quickly termed the bum freezer because of its propensity to ride up the wearer's back. Of course these changes were enthusiastically adopted by the young and completely mystified everyone else. Which was precisely the point.

* * *

'I bought a pink shirt from a shop called Gay Lord. It had a giraffe collar and a tab front. I put it in the wash. The next day I went to get it and I couldn't find it. I said to my mum, "Where's that pink shirt?" She said, "I've torn it up. It's a duster now." I couldn't believe it. I said, "Why?" She said, "Because everyone will think you're a poof." She said, "I'll give you money to buy a new shirt. But please, don't buy pink."'

Carlo Manzi

'My Steve, the first time he wore white trousers out, he was beaten up.'

Kay Marriott – mother of Steve Marriott

'The Mod thing became very hierarchical. There were the people who were into style and then there were the people who were more kind of heavies. They weren't looking for trouble but they didn't dress as smartly. They would wear the clothes we would wear as day wear in the evening. Example. I had a suede jacket, almost like a Levi's, which was grey. I'd wear it at daytime but they would wear it at night time. You always wore a suit at night.'

Ian R. Hebditch

* * *

As 1961 came to a close, a young designer from Scotland, John Stephen, could proudly walk up Carnaby Street and inspect four of his shops. Stephen had started his clothing business back in the mid-'50s in Beak Street, just around the corner. One day he returned to work and found his shop consumed by flames. Undeterred, he regrouped and then opened up again, this time on Carnaby Street. He was up against a lot of competition – Vince's, Adonis – but Stephen – who once told the writer Nik Cohn, 'I want to own more shops than anyone else,' and owned twenty six premises before his luck gave out – quickly started outselling everyone. Shopping was transformed by entrepreneurs such as Stephen. He correctly identified the emergence of the teenager and homed in on his and her wants by creating outlets that were friendly and relaxed. Clothes shops for both sexes sprang up everywhere in London. Often, these shops – Foale and Tuffin, the hugely successful Biba – were brightly decorated and staffed by young people.

The merchandise had a quick turnover. A line of clothes would come in, sell out in a week and rarely be replaced. Success gets noted. Carnaby Street was invaded by journalists. When they started talking about the street as, 'the Mecca for Mods', the true Modernist left it to the tourists and the seven and sixers. They turned their attention to tailors such as Bilgorri in Bishopsgate ('It's a real haddocky place,' Mark Feld told *Town* magazine, 'but he does what you want, all the faces go to Bilgorri.'). Lou Rose in the East End, Jimmy West and David Foley over in Holloway and the famed Sam Arkus in Soho who had been designing boxy tweed jackets since 1955.

* * *

'It was to do with ideas. It was a movement based on ideas, on the idea that an eight-inch vent might be better than a six-inch vent in your jacket. And it was discussed as such. It wasn't that an eight-inch vent was a way of saying, "You haven't got an eight-inch vent and I have." It was actually something you talked about. Was it better to wear your watch on the inside or the outside of your wrist? Which were the best T-shirts to wear under an American shirt? Which ones did and didn't show above the button? Those were the things that mattered. It was creative. It was absolutely creative. It was not in any sense negative.'

Patrick Uden

'I went to Italy – this was when people did not go abroad – and I remember I bought these corduroy shoes and they were the business. Fantastic. I came back, went to whatever gig was on and I was the centre of attention. People crowded round me because of these shoes. In fact, the next night I wore them this Mod became so jealous he tried to stamp on my feet all night.'

Phil Smee

'If you think about sexuality, well in Modernism you dressed for other blokes. You were far more interested in a guy coming up and saying, "Great suit," than a girl coming up and saying, "Great suit." Because the girls didn't look particularly good. Mod girls were never as attractive as Mod boys. They wore clothes that didn't enhance their figures although you would look at a girl if she looked liked she had spent a few bob.'

Carlo Manzi

'As far as the girls went I'd divide them into two categories. There was a group of girls I'd call no-hopers and they would effect what I'd call a loosely masculine style. They'd have short hair, long suede coats, Hush Puppies, ski pants, probably a crewneck jumper. Got on with them fine but didn't think of them as girls. Then there was another group who were much more stylish. You would get the white lipstick, really severe hair cut and they would wear polka dots, white stockings, big plastic jewellery and a very short skirt with a big wide belt on it, like a pelmet skirt. They'd wear shoes with hourglass heels and a lot of them were totally unavailable. They really were, in their own way, very stylish and part of the scene.'

Ian R. Hebditch

'The one fashion I really remember is blue or white hipsters with a slit up the side – these details are very important – a navy blue T-shirt with a target and an anchor in the middle of it, a suede coat, collarless and three-quarter length. Also, I used to buy my trousers from men's shops because they had a much better fit.'

Eileen Barnes – original Mod

'Everything you did was wrong. The music was wrong, the clubs were wrong, the clothes were wrong. I remember getting a friend of mine the sack. She was working in Foyles and I had taken the day off. I was walking down Charing Cross Road with her and everybody was saying, "Look at this girl," and her boss looked out and because she was with me she got the sack. All I was wearing were white tights and a shocking pink mac which I got from Fenwicks.'

Ann Sullivan – original Mod

'I got the sack for wearing my stockings. I used to work for a TV company and I was told I couldn't wear white tights. I couldn't see why that affected my ability to learn anything. So I refused to stop wearing them and I was given the sack.'

Eileen Barnes

'If you didn't go to a boutique or shop run by young people then you went to the other shops where the salespeople would be forty or fifty years old. They'd have dyed hair, lots of lipstick, lots of powder and they hated you.

You'd feel like they thought you had dirty hands and you were touching their merchandise. You didn't want to be there.'

Liz Woodcraft – barrister

'I remember going to John Lewis and buying great big Navy buttons and painting daisies on each one. Then I bought a pair of clip-on earrings, got some daisy flowers and glued them on. We'd wear loads of white make-up, pale lips and then loads of black eye shadow.'

Ann Sullivan

'I used to wear grey eyeliner and mascara. You could only buy small pots of white pearlised stuff and you'd put that on your lips. We all wanted to look like Cathy McGowan (*Ready Steady Go* presenter). We all wanted that Cleopatra look and it was hard because there wasn't anywhere near the kind of hair products which there are nowadays. I read a book by a woman in prison and she said one of the ways that she made her stretch in prison bearable was by having a different hairstyle every day. So I thought, right, that's what I'll do. Sometimes I'd have it parted in the middle and pulled back, other times I'd pin it up.'

Liz Woodcraft

'The focus wasn't on picking up girls but that didn't mean there was no interest in them. Certainly, as far as we were concerned, we'd often go out and because we were from the Birdcage (Portsmouth Mod club) we felt we could more or less have anyone.'

Ian R. Hebditch

'When you were fourteen or fifteen you were desperate to meet a guy who had a driving licence. None of the boys in Cheltenham had passed their test which meant you couldn't go on the back of a scooter. So people would pay 2/6d and if they got stopped they could use their name.'

Liz Woodcraft

THE SOUL STYLISTS

'Mods were not covering their scooters with lights or driving around with little bits of fur at the back. A scooter would be minimal. It would be a GX with chrome buckles, a back carrier and perhaps a fly screen but with nothing written on it. Perhaps a little touch like a fine white line on the tyres and that was it. Also, the idea of parkas . . . I didn't have a parka. I knew people who did have them and they only used them to protect what they had on underneath. They didn't wear them all the time and they didn't write The Who on the back of them. If they did they were scooter boys not Mods.'

Ian R. Hebditch

'In my part of the world, Bromley, which is where I come from, Bromley down in South London there was a Mod down there called Bucket. Now Bucket was quite well known around sort of Finchley and places like that. Because Bucket had a blue pack-a-mac and a blue Vespa and a black beret and no mirrors on his Vespa at all. He'd taken all the chrome off. And he became quite well known for this. In other words it was what he didn't have in a sense that made him exclusive.'

Patrick Uden

'Lawrence Corner was the place to get stuff which I suppose was from the Korean War. I remember at one point the rumour went round that someone had bought a parka there with a silk map lining. The Air Force guys had these parkas and they had whole maps of the area printed on silk lining so if they crashed they would have an extra map. There was a wild rush to get them I know that.'

Phil Smee

'One or two people had parkas but parkas really weren't cool. Everybody thinks that the height of cool was to have an ariel with a fox tail on it and that was so not cool. It was also not cool to have lights all over the front of your scooter. The only thing that mattered was whether you had silver panels or not.'

Liz Woodcraft

'It wasn't uncool. Very few people had good scooters because they couldn't afford it. Very few people had good ones so you did your best to decorate them.'

Phil Smee

'Did I tell you there was a way to ride a scooter? Oh yeah. It was all understatement. You rode it with your feet absolutely straight in. All the emulators rode with their feet sticking out from the platform and they wore Cuban heels. Cuban heels? You don't even talk to them. My parents knew I had a scooter and dressed smart. That was it. It was all nice to them. Don't understand, never going to understand.'

Robert Hall

* * *

THE SOUL STYLISTS

Mods were the first youth cult to customise; that is they took objects and made significant changes to them. Jacket vents were lengthened, trousers altered. Scooters were added to or subtracted from. With their hair styles a similar process took place. Mods took the American Ivy League cut and then added the European touch by insisting on back combing the mane to achieve a bouffant effect. These stylistic shifts were dictated by the faces and transmitted by word of mouth.

Once a trend became evident, it swiftly died only to be immediately replaced by another. But there was one thing the Modernists had no desire to change; and that was the exciting new strands of black music – blues, soul and R&B – that were now pouring into Britain. If Europe and America were dressing the Mod it was black America who was providing the soundtrack. Consequently, in London, the musical policies of many clubs now shifted with the times. Jazz was slowly eased out and the latest R&B records took their place. This move allowed Mods the space to develop the scene. Clubs have always served as vital gathering points, the places where the young converge to check each other out, hear fabulous music and live a twenty-four-hour life. Just like their Modernist predecessors whose Soho streets they now walked upon.

'The Flamingo which was in Wardour Street was run by Jeff and Sam Kruger. Rik Gunnell and Tony Harris ran the all-nighter at the weekends. It still is one of the most exciting experiences of my life walking down those stairs to the Flamingo because there was something about that club, it was so vibrant. I always thought the noise had soaked into the walls. I used to go when Georgie Fame was on which I think was on a weekday. I only went to the all-nighter there a couple of times. I went to the all-nighter at Ronnie Scott's but that was a different kettle of fish because the all-nighter at the Flamingo was quite wild. The black influence was quite strong there and to be honest it was all a bit of a blur. They were playing things like Lord Kitchener's "Dr Kitch" over the PA and Dexter Gordon and Gene Ammonds and Jack McDuff and then ska and bluebeat. This was around 1963 and there weren't DJs in the sense of them talking over the records or announcing them but the records were very exciting and the music was great. Everybody made an effort. It was stylish hair, nice dress, pencil skirts and pale pink lipstick. That was the thing.'

                                                              Val Wilmer

'One night at the Flamingo, in 1964, before we had even started playing, there was a fight between a couple of GIs and one guy got stabbed really badly. The American authorities then put the Flamingo out of bounds. The majority of them came from Chicksands in Cambridgeshire, which was a communication place. But there were guys from all over the country – Greenham Common, Furford in Gloucestershire. The all-nighter for them was home from home. It was the only place where black American GIs could hang out, dance and get out of it. By midnight, when the club opened, most of them were out of it. They would have left the base late afternoon, got on the train with a bottle of something and by the time they came into the club they would be raving.' Anyway, the Flamingo was put off-limits and the next week the Mods came in. And they loved what they were doing.'

                                                              Georgie Fame

'First of all you'd go to the Discotheque (Wardour Street) and you got your hand stamped. There used to be a shop on Wardour Street that had a fluorescent light and you could check to see if you had the same stamp as the Scene and then if you had, you could go to both clubs.'

Ann Sullivan

'You would wander between the Scene and the Discotheque. There were always people around to talk to. Then you'd find out that there was a new group coming to play The Marquee. So you'd go up there and you would stay until the end and then because it was too late to go home and too early to do anything else, you would go and have breakfast. Then a little ride round on the Circle line before you went home and in my case on to Mass.'

Eileen Barnes

'You never went to the Whiskey-A-Go-Go (above the Flamingo on Wardour Street). because it was full of foreign students. We went to the opening of the Scene (in Ham Yard) and it became our club. The Stones used to turn up now and again because the best bands played there. Duffy Powell and the Fifth Dimension was the best R&B band this country has ever produced and no one remembers them. He used to play there and he was a real great singer. Anyway, one night The Stones show up with a bunch of wankers with funny suits on. We were outside doing a bit of dealing, looking over at them and saying, "Who are those dicks?" George Harrison and John Lennon is who they are. After that, we wouldn't leave them alone.'

Chris Hill

'Rik Gunnell who used to run the Flamingo was a bit shady and the blokes who ran The Discotheque were decidedly shady. We knew people who knew that crowd and so every now and then you'd go to one of these clubs and meet these heavy-duty guys. We were very impressed.'

Ann Sullivan

'We opened the Roaring Twenties. That was a great club. It was mainly a West Indian club where a few black GIs used to go, whereas the Flamingo was really a black American place where a few WI's used to go. There were a couple of Jewish guys that Rik knew and they had this property on Carnaby Street which they wanted to turn into a dance club, mainly for young Jewish kids from Finchley Road. Rik said, all right, we'll put the band in. We opened it one night and it was packed with young, white kids. The next week it was totally empty, nobody went. The first night they had invited everyone in for a freebie and of course the next time no one went. Then Count Suckle turned up on the scene. Suckle was the original West Indian disc jockey and he used to come down the Flamingo all-nighters. Suckle was looking for a place and when he heard about the club he just said, "Well, I can fill it with my people." Suckle took it over and we opened it. It was a big Jamaican party. We played the Sunday all-nighter for several months. Suckle had this fantastic source for music. He had this guy in Memphis who sent him all the new American soul records and he also had a Jamaican connection so he had all the latest records. So it was Suckle and the American GIs bringing in records to the Flamingo, that was our source for all this music. The first records we made as a band were Ska songs, we did a version of Orange Street. We also backed a couple of West Indian singers. I can't remember their names but that was for Bluebeat Records. Before that the first recording I ever did on an organ was with Prince Buster on an album called Soul Of Africa, which I think was in 1963. I met Buster down the Roaring Twenties. That was the Jamaican community in the West End.'

Georgie Fame

'James Hamilton was the DJ at the Scene and he was brilliant. Amazing records.'

Chris Hill

'And of course you mustn't forget Guy Stevens. He was the DJ at the Scene and he was really important. He was the person importing all the black music and he had the most amazing record collection. We used to go round to his house and he was a total speed freak but he was a genius. He had thousands of records and you'd go round and just play them all night. Very early on we had discovered this club called Klooks Kleek up the road in West Hampstead. It was above a pub called the Railway Hotel. They played the most amazing black music. The thing is nobody was famous then. Everybody played up there. The Steampacket, Graham Bond, Zoot Money. I saw Stevie Wonder there when he was Little Stevie Wonder and he was fantastic.'

Ann Sullivan

* * *

THE SOUL STYLISTS

Sixties American R&B music – as it does to this day – had no difficulty in winning lifelong admirers. The strand of it known as soul had emerged in 1955 when Ray Charles, the blind singer-songwriter that many considered a genius, started adapting gospel-style music for his own means. He did this by putting – in producer Jerry Wexler's memorable phrase – the Devil's words to the Lord's music. Charles removed gospel's devotional lyrics and added words of love and lust, desire and want, to a music that was unknown outside of black churches in America. The effect of Charles' work was immediate. First of all it split the church community in two and, like many of the decade's most vital issues, the argument over the validity and morality of his actions raged between the young and the old. Secondly, records such as his 'What I'd Say', propelled numerous young performers towards a new direction. Independent labels – such as Berry Gordy's Motown operation in Detroit and older outfits such as Atlantic Records in New York City – enthusiastically opened up their doors to this music. Soon a million other entrepreneurs in America followed suit, seeking the huge riches that the record business bestows on only the few.

Soul groups were formed on a daily basis, many of which viewed the industry as a definitive way out of their poor economic condition. The sound was fresh, exciting and for white British kids, glamorous beyond belief. Most of what America produced was tinged with magic because in the early '60s, America really was another world, proud, imperious, fascinating and totally inaccessible to most people.

The performers the Mods admired appeared before them on record sleeves and in newspaper pictures wearing sharply cut mohair suits, button-down shirts and tight three-button jackets with a hanky stuffed in the top pocket.

Mods thrilled to these images. They saw themselves reflected in them. More than this, soul music now began to inspire the new generation of young British groups struggling to be heard within an indifferent music business. The Beatles, the first group to write their own songs and revolutionise the music business, adored Motown. They covered its songs ('Twist and Shout' by The Isleys being the most notable in their early days), and they name-checked as many artists as they could in interviews. In London, a whole generation of musicians – Zoot Money, Graham Bond – all began working towards establishing a British R&B sound. Yet despite their efforts and hip success, few of them truly impressed the Modernists. Which wasn't surprising. Modernists were purists. They wanted the real thing, not the imitation. So very few British musicians got the nod.

But Georgie Fame did. In 1962, this young Lancashire lad and his band the Blue Flames secured a night at the Flamingo's all-nighter. It was March 1962. By September of the same year, Rik Gunnell was managing Georgie who, to no one's surprise, had now been given a residency at Rik's Flamingo all-nighters. Soon an album, *Rhythm and Blues From The Flamingo* was recorded and released. By which time Georgie, having been exposed to the likes of Mose Allison, Jimmy Smith and Richard 'Groove' Holmes, had switched from piano to Hammond organ and extended his repertoire to include Motown, soul, modern jazz, R&B and the newly emerging ska music. Well dressed and possessor of a silky, smooth voice which never sounded forced or strained no matter what material he was covering, Fame's taste and style was given the nod by even the most ardent of

Modernists. It was some achievement. Other groups emerged from the Mod scene, all of them – The Small Faces, The Action, The Art Woods – authentic Mods and totally enamoured with black music. But the Mod cognoscenti were totally divided as to their worth.

* * *

'The big live bands of the era were Geno Washington, Mike Cotton Sound, Georgie Fame, The Artwoods, Zoot Money. We liked these bands because of the covers they did. Later on, The Small Faces, I felt, were the real deal as well as The Action. And Amen Corner – people forget how good they were. The Alan Bown Set were brilliant. The thing about the Mods is that they were into a lot of shit. They were into the Beach Boys. The Beach Boys were a big Mod band – I don't give a fuck what anyone says.'

Chris Hill

'I totally rejected The Beatles. It was only later on that I started seeing the value of them. They were a pop phenomenon but that was nothing to do with us. The only bands we were into were Tamla inspired – The Action, for example or The Move, they were really sound because they played Tamla stuff. Other groups we liked would be The Art Woods, Geno Washington, Herbie Goines and the Nightriders, the Paramounts. The trouble with groups such as The Small Faces is that they tended to attract a girl teenybopper audience which we were never comfortable with. They were a bit too mainstream for us. As for Tamla music it was not mainstream Tamla we liked but the more obscure stuff. We weren't interested in The Supremes but The Marvellettes, now that was a whole different ballgame. Smokey Robinson was all right, Marvin as well. What we wanted was the hard amphetamine stuff of Jimmy James and the Vagabonds. People like Georgie Fame I enjoyed but he was too mellow. We wanted something that had a real buzz to it like, "Boogaloo Party" by The Olympics.'

Ian R. Hebditch

'In those days you would buy virtually anything on Stax and virtually anything on Motown because you knew it would be good. Atlantic was very much a black music label as was Chess records with its Chicago blues sound. And that's where the variety came in. It wasn't between slow and fast, it was between the funkier sounds of Stax or the orchestrated sounds of Motown.'

David Cole

'You never really bought English records – a bit uncool. Also, for the first time you'd hear records in shops and you never had that before. It was probably the first time there was record plugging. If you could get your records into John Stephen's shops you were laughing.'

Carlo Manzi

'People used to walk around with records under their arms. It was the ultimate in posing. My friend John used to carry Carla Thomas and Otis Redding's *King & Queen* album under his arm. That was his badge, his calling card.'

Phil Smee

'I would say that Rod Stewart was fairly highly thought of, obviously Pete Townsend, Steve Marriott. But there was no way that you'd ever emulate them because they weren't really perceived as Mods. When they were in a band they couldn't keep looking as sharp because a lot of the time they would be onstage sweating and their clothes would be ruffled.'

Ian R. Hebditch

* * *

Another musical strand to emerge and then delight the Mod sensibility was bluebeat music or ska as it would later be known. The music was established through Britain's slowly expanding Jamaican communities, its journey starting in 1954 when Duke Vin set up the UK's first Jamaican sound system. Later on, musicians such as Ernest Ranglin the guitarist or trombonist Rico Rodriguez played with the likes of Georgie Fame at the Flamingo. Other musicians emerged. Singers such as Jackie Edwards (composer of 'Keep On Running' for the Spencer Davis group), Derrick Morgan and the mighty Prince Buster, all found success with their expatriate countrymen and the Mods.

* * *

'Prince Buster told me this story once that after a gig he was being driven home through some rough part of London and he wanted to stop by a roadside café and get a cup of tea. Whoever was with him was saying, no man, it's too rough round here. But Buster said, "Man, I am from Kingston in Jamaica. What's going to frighten me?" So he got out, went up and asked for a cup of tea and just as he did these white guys suddenly appeared next to him and started talking to him because they loved the cut of his Brooks Brothers-type suit. They were Mods and Prince Buster became a huge Mod hero. They used to give him a scooter escort out of towns he had just played. That's a fact.'

Lloyd Bradley

* * *

With their pork-pie hats, American sharkskin suits and overall neat appearance, Jamaican performers won unanimous approval. Mods were open-minded. Not narrow.

* * *

'There was a great degree of respect between the Mods and the West Indian community. I personally found that. Within the Mod movement I don't recollect any element of racism at all and by racism I mean anti-black feeling.'

Ian R. Hebditch

* * *

In August of 1963, Rediffusion TV started their new pop programme, *Ready Steady Go*. Transmitted on a Friday night as the entire teenage world prepared to go out, the show's slogan – 'Here comes the weekend' – and its pop-art ethos instantly caught the spirit of the times. *Ready Steady Go* had two unique features. Bands were allowed to play live and its teenage audience was carefully hand picked from Mod central clubs such as the Scene or Klooks Kleek Klub. Consequently, *Ready Steady Go* instantly staked out its own territory. The show often put on unknown acts. It displayed no qualms in allowing Paul Jones to sing Bob Dylan's, 'With God On Our Side' despite a BBC ban on the song. It used young presenters – Cathy McGowan who quickly became a teen icon – and Patrick Kerr who showed off the new dances. But its most important function was to take Mod culture out of the London club scene and into every home in Britain. *Ready Steady Go* nationalised Mod. It showed a kid in Manchester not only what his London counterpart was wearing but more importantly, how he was styling his clothes.

* * *

'I danced on *Ready Steady Go* for a year I suppose. I was filmed every four to six weeks. I had a passport (issued to regulars to allow them swift entry into the studios based in Kingsway, Holborn). It happened because I was at the Scene once – actually I was mucking around with a girlfriend of mine – and that young guy Patrick came in with somebody and said, "Would you like to go on *Ready Steady Go* as one of the dancers? You can go on the special dancing slot." And who fluffed it? Me! I can dance fine but I can't do it with people looking at me. Anyway, I survived it. Basically, you had to look good, mingle with the crowd and dance away. I remember Cathy McGowan coming up to me and saying, "Oh I love your shoes. They're really fab." I remember where I got them, Elliott on Bond Street. They were white with strips of colour going across the top.'

Ann Sullivan

'I swear to God I was the first person to wear a pork pie hat on *Ready Steady Go*. What I had was this Frank Sinatra hat that I had cut the brim off which I wore in the audience. That week Georgie Fame was on and so were the Ronnettes. The show was recorded live and later that night I went to a dance at Thames Boardmill and when I got there they got me up onstage saying, "It's the star from *Ready Steady Go!*" Talk about instant stardom.'

Chris Hill

* * *

Ready Steady Go taught the nation's teenagers what to wear, how to wear it. Just by studying the audience you could tune into the new look. Musically, as time went by, the show's spotlight tended to fall more and more upon soul artists.

There were specials on Otis Redding and the Motown label, hosted by one of soul's biggest fans, the singer Dusty Springfield. *Ready Steady Go* gladly exposed this music just as it gladly displayed new dances to its keen viewers. For many enthusiasts this was a crucial element of the show. Watching the dancers gave them a real sense of anticipation for the night's intake of chemicals. For make no mistake, Mods loved amphetamines. The small blue pills they swallowed – SmithKline and French with the line down the middle were regarded as the finest – gave them confidence, energy and power. For dancing, for styling, for talking, for pleasure, amphetamines have fuelled every Mod-related cult until the late '80s.

* * *

THE SOUL STYLISTS

'In the clubs you danced all the time. Non-stop. In fact, you were far more likely to remember the moments when you didn't dance because they played a crap record. That's why you needed the pills, the energy. The Scene was a fabulous club and it was the easiest place to get pills as well. You know people say, well you take a handful and bung them down your neck? Well, it was literally like that.'

Carlo Manzi

'The whole idea of amphetamines comes from an American culture. The American soldiers used to take them to stay awake, bomber pilots and so on, it was well known that soldiers took drugs in order to remain awake. Through the American beat culture – it came through that.'

Patrick Uden

'The drugs were crucially important. First of all they were cheap. Sixpence for a blue. Blues were really in favour, the ones with a line down the middle. For a good night out it was essential because otherwise you couldn't get the right head on. You couldn't keep dancing and dancing was absolutely crucial. There was a lot of naivety about what the effects were and what was meant to happen and some people suffered very badly by overindulging. They went a bit strange by going at it too hard, too long. They were out of their heads all week whereas for most of us it was weekends. And just a little bit during the week. Dick Hebidge said the Mods were the undead and I think that was very perceptive.

'You talked in these clipped tones and you hung around coffee bars waiting for something to happen and all the time, depending on what day of the week it was, you were either coming up or coming down. And it was the change in drugs that helped change the whole Mod thing.'

Ian R. Hebditch

* * *

According to Denzil, the Mod that the *Sunday Times* featured in their 2 August edition of 1964, 'pills made you edgy and argumentative.' Certainly, by now, the stylists, the faces, were feeling uncertain. Thanks to television such as *Ready Steady Go*, the introduction of pirate radio (Ronan O'Rahilly who owned The Scene had started Radio Caroline that year which broadcast a mix of pop and soul from its position in the North Sea. One of its effects was to popularise Mod music), the proliferation of boutiques and shops catering to the young, the emergence of groups such as The Who (which Mod-obsessed Pete Meaden had used to give Mod culture national exposure) there was a growing feeling that their way of life was under threat. National recognition had not helped serve the Mod cause. It had helped to dilute it. So when the national papers reported on beach fights between Mods and Rockers taking place in various seaside resorts in that summer of 1964, the Modernist had already read the writing on the wall. He and she slipped from view. And stayed there.

* * *

'I would say that the Mod thing lasted between 1962 and 1964 because 1965 was really Beatles time plus you had those beach fights and it was nothing to do with that.'

Eileen Barnes

'Modernism was eclectic, it crossed everything. It brought blues music into contact with car design, car design into contact with fashion, fashion design into contact with food. We are used to having stuff imported into this country. We're great bringers-in of things. And this is largely due, I think, to the positivism that existed then. That it was worth bringing something in and having a good look at it. We like that. You know.'

Patrick Uden

'I think it was the first real generation gap. It doesn't exist now as it did then but there was a massive gap. People who were 19 looked really old to us and their parents were absolutely Victorian. I think that one thing alone led to so much more creativity.'

Phil Smee

* * *

Modernism has remained Britain's most enduring youth cult because its originators created a blueprint that has proved timeproof. By doing so, they knowingly put up a safeguard against the transient nature of fashion. Mod has never withered against the ravages of time because Mod is so particular. About everything. Detail is all. Mod created, for the very first time, a twenty-four-hour lifestyle that totally revolved around fashion, music, drugs and attitude. They did so because Mods were working-class smart. They did not oppose society, they simply ignored it. They created their own secret sign language, devised fashion codes and style statements, developed, in fact, their very own culture of cool. That they kept themselves hidden from view did not stop them contributing heavily towards the society they ignored. Their demands for clothes and music literally laid the foundations for those industries in Britain and their style demanded a complete shift in attitude towards menswear. The true Modernist transformed London. He made it hip-central. Mod clubs were the best in town. Mod DJs played the best and most exciting records and Mods danced the best dances.

All this because Mods had no problem mixing other cultures into their own. Mods were many things – arrogant, contemptuous, cruel, peacocks to a man, but they were always open-minded and ambitious. One of their credos was simple; if it's good – take it, wherever it's from. Consequently, Mod musical taste was immaculate and its development is entwined with the history of soul music's triumphant entry into Britain. Which is how Mod musical taste changed the capital's club scene. Best of all, when it was time to leave the party, quietly and elegantly, true Mods did so without a

THE SOUL STYLISTS

murmur. They simply vanished. Which is so perfectly right, so perfectly Modernist.

* * *

'By the time Cathy McGowan came on TV it was all over. You might as well have drawn the curtains. If that was the date, 1963, then that was when it died. I think the original Mods were quite happy to see themselves emulated on television but when that spread nationally it was finished.'

Robert Hall

'First of all it was a sense that you created your own beliefs and that other people were not very relevant at all. If other people weren't carrying certain badges they were totally irrelevant. You didn't want to harm them. They just didn't matter. The only people who had anything of any validity to say were those who shared your beliefs. There was this sense that you were right but you were constantly moving on and breaking new ground. You didn't want to stay where you are. You lived for the moment or maybe for tomorrow at a push. There was no long-term planning. Instead, there was a kind of optimism that it was going to go on forever; that you would always be on top of the heap.'

Ian R. Hebditch

CHAPTER THREE

THE BUTTON-DOWN TYPES

'In this country working-class people don't take things from the middle classes, they take it from America and then they twist it round. Which is why no one can work out where The Look originates from.'

James Ferguson – illustrator

* * *

MODERNISTS DON'T DIE. They just give themselves away to the new when they felt too old. It was their younger brothers and sisters who carried on the tradition. In the mid-'60s, if you were young and working-class, you were either a Mod or you were a nobody. And it was from this period that a new youth cult – sharp and uncompromising – would have its genesis. For three years it had no name, but what this generation signified – consciously or not – was a total rejection of the unstyled masses brawling on the beaches and a true return to the Mod principles of exclusivity and secrecy.

The most striking element of this new leaner look was the cropped haircut, taken from the American GI and deliberately used to shock, subvert and frighten. Not only did this severe cut succeed in its mission but it also served a dual purpose by uniting the differing clothing styles that were now appearing all over the capital. For example, in West London

– Acton, Chiswick and stretching out to Harrow in the North West – the Mods favoured the Ivy League style. There are reasons enough for this choice but one of them was the close proximity of the Ivy Shop in Richmond, which specialised in imported American clothing.

Moving across London and into the inner city areas, the style differed. It was here that the Rude Boy look, which had emanated from Jamaica and was based on the Ivy League look, now asserted itself as second-generation Carib-beans moved deeper into British society. For the very first time, West Indian fashion would now play a major part in influencing young British street fashion. Braces, pork-pie hats and the return of the Crombie coat, were some of the clothing items that were taken from the Rude Boy by his white counterpart.

In tandem with this increased influence, Jamaican music now came into its own through the success of performers such as Prince Buster. By slowing down its frenetic beat, ska had now transformed itself into rock steady and with labels such as Stax, Atlantic and Motown still operating at the height of their powers, this musical mix – reggae got soul! – became the soundtrack for the new breed.

In 1967, many teenage wardrobes consisted of – amongst other items – Ben Sherman shirts, Fred Perry tops, Dormeuil Tonik suits, Levi jeans, red socks, loafer shoes. But it was the adoption of the closely cropped haircut – triggering a series of nicknames such as peanut, baldhead, boiled egg, which echoed down London's streets – that unified the participants. It was only when the *Daily Mirror* newspaper used the word Skinhead, on 3 September, 1969, in an article headlined, 'No Love From Johnny', did this movement finally find itself christened. By then, however, the smartness of the original look had been usurped for a much more functional and populist style that consisted of boots, braces, button-down shirts and Harrington jackets. As with the Modernist movement of the early '60s, the media had picked up on the tail-end of the movement. The result was that the extreme care and style that had gone into the making of the Skinhead was crucially missed in favour of lurid stories concerning violence, racist behaviour and outright thuggery.

Just as the original Mods were destined to be remembered by spurious

THE SOUL STYLISTS

Bank Holiday anniversaries, so the Skinhead has been commemorated for his anger rather than his original, exquisite style.

* * *

'I was walking along Great Yarmouth going to see a band and I said to my mates, "Look at these Mods here, they've all got their hair very short now." That was in July 1967. They'd cut their hair very close, like a neater Mod not a Skinhead cut as you might know it. I remember saying, "This is a different kind of Mod." And it was moving in. But the funny thing about the Skinheads was that they didn't like rock'n'roll music. You had the people that were Mods and grew their hair and turned into hippies. And the ones that didn't want to do that turned Skinhead and went into reggae.'

Jesse Hector – musician

'The influence came from West London. I remember I went on holiday and I met a girl from South East London and I don't think it was strong over there as it was over West London. I am pretty sure it was more West. That said, there weren't that many pukka Skinheads in Harrow where I lived. It was more a thing with the blokes from Acton, Ealing, Chiswick and possibly a few in Wealdstone.

See, I always said Skinheads were Mods. The papers gave them the name Skinheads but in my heart they were Mods. Mods had different styles. Regency style, this style, that style. This was another style. Now don't forget, just before the changeover, the Mods were wearing bomber jackets with elastic collars and they had college-boy haircuts which isn't far off the Skinhead. The start of it was geezers wearing Cherry Red boots. So the bomber jacket became a Harrington, the jeans stayed the same or some went onto Sta-prest. I remember the ones that liked the rucking had the bomber jackets on and the boots. It was rucking gear that they felt comfortable in. But the original Skinheads wore American clothes. Right from the beginning, it was all American clothes, trying to look like Yanks.

THE SOUL STYLISTS

81

I was sixteen at the time. Then the next thing I noticed was that it started changing from the mohair – which they got from the Mod. I think a lot of the clothes came from the Mods. If you look at the Mod clothes, they might not have been wearing Sta-prest but they were wearing different coloured slacks and that was what Sta-prest were.'

Terry Wheeler – fashion consultant

* * *

According to musician Kevin Rowland's essay, '1969 and what the Media called the Skinheads', the style came directly from Mod culture. He recalls the phrase, 'Top Mod' often being employed as a compliment. He recalls the Mods in his area of Harrow sporting items such as long gaberdine, single-breasted, fly-fronted raincoats, V-neck lambs wool sweaters, parallel trousers with pleats, MA flying jackets with elasticated cuffs and collar, Levi 501 jeans, made to measure suit jackets with three buttons, single vented, waisted with not only a breast pocket but three other pockets with sloping flaps. In terms of hairstyles, the college boy haircut was easily the most prevalent.

The popularity of this look signalled a decline in Europe's fashion influence and another surge in popularity for the evergreen Ivy League look. Another major American influence was the military look. This sharp style had fascinated so many British people when they were exposed to it, either on their own streets or in flickering, darkened cinemas.

* * *

'There was a film called *Countdown* that came out in about 1967. It was one of Robert Duvall's first films and James Caan's as well. It was about astronauts and they dressed in white button-down collar shirts, trousers that looked like Sta-prest and they had haircuts which anyone English would recognise as a pure Skinhead cut.'

George Georgiou – interior designer

'A mate of mine at school said he had bought this LP at the weekend just for the cover. It was a photograph of Frank Sinatra with a slim-brim pork-pie hat, worn at an angle, a button-down shirt with the top button undone, a tie and a suit. We didn't care about the music, just the way he looked. We thought, yes. Another one was Lee Marvin in the film *Point Blank* wearing a suit and Royals.'

James Ferguson

* * *

A massive American base, located on the outskirts of West London in Ruislip, was undoubtedly a contributory factor to the fashion shapes of West London. But if anyone was responsible for the ongoing popularisation of American clothing in Britain from the mid-'60s onwards, it was the clothes proprietor John Simon. In 1965, he and his business partner, Jeff Kwintner, opened the Ivy Shop in Richmond. It is a name that will resonate for many. The shop was a massive underground success but not in the way that its owners had first envisaged. John Simon was an East End child who fell in love with clothes at a very early age. Initially, American clothing dazzled him. Then it became his inspiration and driving force.

* * *

'During the war the GIs based here were really glamorous to us and that's because their uniforms were made out of gabardine whilst the British troops all wore heavy shapeless woollen clothes. So of course the Americans looked so much smarter with their polished shoes and well cut trousers. I remember as a kid in the East End, we would go up to the GIs and say, "Got any gum, chum?"'

John Simon

* * *

Setting out on his own in the '60s, Simon's vision was simple. He wanted to popularise the Ivy League look in Britain. He loved The Look and like all obsessives he wanted to share his passion with the rest of the country.

* * *

'In 1960 there were not that many shops selling American clothing. There was David's on Charing Cross Road which was an important shop. They had been selling USA clothing since the late '40s. They based their look on a 1930s American shop. It was full of green marble and chrome and had an art deco look. They sold Lion of Troy shirts and Pendletons which are shirts made of pure wool. Then there was Cecil Gee and Austins, which was a very special shop. For the Modernists it had a great impact. Then there were other shops like Davis's in the East End or Gray's in Dalston. These were shops that would sell menswear but in slightly watered down American styles.

As for us, in 1962–63 we used to sell clothes in Petticoat Lane, stuff like polka-dot tab-collar shirts and Paisley shirts. One of the makers of the clothes we sold had a little entrance to his shop and we got him to let us use the entrance as a little shop. That was called Clothesville. Then me and a friend, Jeff Kwintner, joined together. We had very meagre finance but with it we opened the Ivy Shop in Richmond. If it hadn't taken money in the first week we would have gone under. Luckily, people came in straight away and that's how the Ivy Shop started. This was 1965. The address was 10 Hill Rise, Richmond, Surrey. The number was 940 9378.'

John Simon

* * *

At first, John's intended market was young British executive types, making their way in Britain's booming industries. He wanted them to dress like their American counterparts.

'We were looking for the young executive around town, that American *Playboy* magazine thing. It was that whole lifestyle – having stereos, nice objects, amazing gadgets. But it didn't turn out like that. More and more younger people got interested in our stock and that's how it became famous. We had queues outside. I would say it was the most influential shop of the '60s. If people are hip they talk about it. If people are treading a slightly dodgy line then they don't talk about it.'

John Simon

* * *

The Ivy Shop created their own clothes. A shirt maker in Walthamstow supplied them with their own Albany line which they sold through the shop. Then a chance meeting gave Simon the key to his later success.

* * *

'The first button-down shirts we had from America were called Tigers Foot and they were made by Dickies, but not the Dickies you know today. This is how it happened. We were in the shop one day and this Porsche drew up outside the shop and this young American executive got out. Jeff Flood was his name and he was wearing the total Ivy League look. He had been sent over by Dickies to check out Europe. He said, "I've got these shirts here." We went, "What!" It was exactly what we had been looking for. He became our good friend then. He was always coming into the shop because we bought everything he had. He used to give us these shirts in packs of four, tied up with string. The collars were quite small, not unlike the Ralph Lauren collar.'

John Simon

'We always called them Ivy jackets. Even after *Peyton Place* started and people started calling them Harringtons, we never did. They were always Ivy jackets.'

Terry Wheeler

THE SOUL STYLISTS

The first brand of shoes the Ivy Shop sold were Timpson's brogues, usually known as Royals. They also sold other versions of the shoe known as plain caps and wingtips.

* * *

'The reason they were called wingtips was because they had a wider rim than English brogues. There were plain caps which had no pattern on them. They used to shine up like glass. There were Gibsons with a rim on the top. They were made in Northampton to American specifications, shipped over there and then shipped back again. You could buy English brogues but they were not the same. They had no rim on them.'

Terry Wheeler

'The best Royals were made of cordovan (horse leather) and I got a pair on Kilburn High Road. I went down for a wedding and snuck out and got this maroon pair which were the most expensive. The smell! It was like sniffing a drug. I couldn't stop.'

James Ferguson

'I'm from Slough and I remember Johnny and Billy Robinson. Their dad was a bit of a face and they all had Royals shoes. One of them bought a pair and they were too small for him so my mum bought them with her Bingo winnings, £2.50 or something. They were smooths, they were fantastic and they were too small for me. I still wore them for three years, though. Both of my toes have got bunions now.'

Terry Farley – DJ

* * *

A little later loafers were put on sale in the Ivy Shop – penny loafers (featuring coins which American students used to slip into the shoe for luck) or the popular fringe tasselled or just plain.

The raincoats were British made and fly fronted with Peter Pan collars and raglan sleeves. This clothing soon attracted a young, mixed clientele. But they weren't the executive types that John originally sought. These were young, working-class kids obsessed with style and who spoke a new language. He remembers his young black customers referring to brogues as, 'blockbusters' and loafers as 'canoes' because of their boat-like shape.

* * *

'It wasn't a very big shop. It had a wooden floor, which was unusual for that time, so it looked oldie oldie. I think they were going for what was known as the New England look which was an American interior style based on a British look. They had glass cabinets in the front with a few bits and pieces in them and behind that racks and racks of shirts. There were tables with shoes all the way down the middle of the shop. There was always a tailor's dummy with a jacket or a shirt on it.'

Terry Wheeler

* * *

But there were other factors to take into consideration.

In 1967, Enoch Powell made his famous inflammatory speech concerning immigration. Powell was a worried, misguided, reactionary man, his anxiety triggered by the number of Caribbean families that had now settled in Britain. He transmitted his concerns by using emotive metaphors, warning of the 'rivers of blood' that would flow on the streets of England thanks to the Caribbean presence. The next day, after his inevitable sacking, the dockers took to those very same streets to march in support of his prophecy.

Against their and Powell's wishes, Britain was turning into a multicultural society. A sizeable number of Caribbean families, pooling their finances and selling on now-owned property, were carefully watching their children assimilate into British society. For the first time, second-generation blacks now mixed with their white counterparts, the two groups heavily influencing each other in the areas of fashion and music. It was a healthy mix, although ironically it was taking place against the backdrop of an escalating immigration battle.

Bowing to public pressure, a Labour government had started a policy of restriction on entry into the UK. Culturally, this meant that second-generation Caribbeans were cut off from their natural home and its influences. Where fashions might have travelled from New York to Jamaica and then into Britain through the arrival of family members, new styles now took much longer to make the third part of the journey.

At this juncture, many second-generation Caribbean youths sported the classic Mod look, but with slightly different details. Trousers were Sta-prest but worn shorter. Ties would be displayed, but with the top shirt button undone. This was in keeping with tradition. Jamaica had been swamped in American culture and heavily influenced by its music.

The premier outfit at this time were The Impressions. When this Curtis Mayfield-led group visited the island for the first time, the crowd reaction at the airport was akin to that of the Beatles landing in America. The Impressions added to reggae's musical depth and history. Their influence could be heard in the harmony sound of many reggae groups, such as The Heptones, who adopted it for their own use. Image-wise, their influence was equally strong. An early press shot of Bob Marley's group The Wailers found them wearing shiny mohair suits and adopting a pose directly taken from an Impressions' *Greatest Hits* album cover. Again, the Ivy League look was the template.

This style was adopted by young ghetto teenagers who called themselves Rude Boys. The Rude Boy emerged around 1964, triggering off a period of political violence in Jamaica which badly scarred its towns and villages. The two main political parties – the JLP and the PNP – turned a blind eye to this intimidation carried out on their behalf, but the reggae records of the time were quick to mythologise the Rude Boy. Soon, his influence was felt in London.

* * *

'In 1968, when I was 13 years old, I was wearing narrow-cut trousers with little turn-ups and worn at half mast, red socks – which were very important – Gabicci suede-fronted jumpers with large collars and two pockets, and my hair would be short with a razor parting which was a Jamaican style that came about because of the heat. It was called a Rude Boy style and it was almost translated wholesale into skinhead dress. The way we wore our trousers, for instance. We wore them high above our ankles, which Mods didn't and which skinheads did. Also, look at the Crombie.

In the suits we wore, the jacket was often three-quarter length. It came down to our knees. Then the skinheads adopted Crombies, which was the exact same look but in a heavier material because it is so bloody cold here. See, at this point there was a real cultural interchange going on. There were kids who grew up on the same estates, went to the same schools, and they crossed over. Not only with fashions, either. In the same way that Mods were into Stax, Motown and Soul, these kids were into Motown, Soul and reggae.'

Lloyd Bradley

'It was only when the offspring of the first-generation parents found themselves neither Jamaican or English that they developed their own culture which took inspiration from both English and Jamaican culture. That's when they became glamour figures for the young white kids.'

John Simon

'There's a story about the singer Desmond Dekker coming to England to play a gig and being given a suit to perform in. He then cut the trouser length by about six or seven inches and went onstage and the day after, everybody was wearing their strides like him. That's a true story. Now, I'm from North London and in the '60s, essentially, you shopped locally. No one went down the West End. You didn't know what the West End was. It was more local things. Like Burtons was a big deal. That's where everyone I know got their first suit made. You got a made-to-measure suit there. I remember mine was brown and black tonik, three buttons, long centre vent – the longer the better – and two pockets, narrow-cut trousers and braces. You didn't wear a belt, you wore braces, but under your shirt because you wore your shirt outside your trousers. Polo shirts got big, but Gabicci was the thing, especially a suede-fronted one. Hats were always a big deal. They weren't quite trilbies but they had a narrow brim. The thing about Burtons is that they used to put tables outside with books of their samples on them. We'd nick them and then sell the material at school as mohair handkerchiefs.'

Lloyd Bradley

'The whole scene was highly influenced by black culture, the haircut, the length of our trousers, the walk, the dances, some of the talk and of course the music. Much of it was copied from the Rude Boy style. Black and white generally got on well together, intermingled – and if there was trouble, it would be about women.'

Nigel Mann – original skinhead

* * *

For many West Londoners, the Ivy Shop was easily accessible which accounts for the Ivy look spreading all over this part of the capital. In other areas of the capital, a slightly different look was being shaped. This was a harder, more stripped-down version of the West London model.

* * *

'I was born in January, 1951 at Barts Hospital in Smithfield. This makes me a genuine Cockney. Dad in Navy, mum in factory. Raised on council estate opposite Arsenal Football ground, Elwood Street, N5. At this time the Mod scene was at its height. I was a young teenager already interested in music. One of my aunts had given me an old Dansette and some early R&B tunes. I also remember seeing really smart geezers on scooters, 1965–66. I was still at school but I had two part-time jobs in Jamaican grocery shops. I can remember three of us at school in Hackney (me, Dave Arnold, Bob Nelson) reading *Exchange and Mart* looking at how cheap scooters were. There were loads of them but we never bought one because it was starting to die out. All the Highbury Mods got white Austen champs, like a Range Rover, and they would leave their old scooters in the tram sheds. We ended up making them go and learning how to drive them.

I was fascinated by the Mod thing. Mods seemed to have money, clothes, music, girls and they had this swagger. I was a young impressionable teenager. We had this little clique at school that was into black music. Tamla, Stax, Atlantic. Most other kids were Beatle or Rolling Stone heads. In September 1967, one of the boys, my mate Dave, came back from Spain with his mum, dad and sister. Fuck me he was nearly bald. Turns out he had met two lads from Plaistow – Sean and Paul – who told him about this new look. You can't imagine the effect this had. While other kids were brushing their hair forward thinking they were the Monkees there were now three baldies in their midst. Teachers used to shake their heads in disbelief. I left school in December, 1967. I can't remember the trigger for rock steady music but I must have heard it at a party or something. I just know that I loved it (still do) and the first rock steady record I bought was "Move Up" by Al and the Vibrators on Doctor Bird, still got it. Most of us had now started work – January 1968 – apprenticeships, Smithfield market, labourers etc. So we started to buy records, clothes and pills.

I know of other Skinheads from different parts of London that didn't take drugs but in Hackney there were plenty that did. The Chesham Arms on a Friday night – straight from work, twenty blues, four a pound. Then home, dinner, bath, get changed, five blues on the bus so by the time I got to the Tottenham Royal I was buzzing, along with many of the other Skins there. We never had any bother chatting the girls up as we all could have talked for England and if you had shares in Wrigley's chewing gum you would have been laughing all the way to the bank.

You didn't get much reggae at dance halls in those days. It was Tamla, Stax and Atlantic and things like, "Cop A Groove" by Bobby Wells, "Mellow Moonlight" by Roy Docker, "African Velvet" by Black Velvet, "The Pearl" by Jerry O and "60 Minutes Of Your Love" by Homer Banks. I can't understand why reggae wasn't played because when "Sufferer" by The Kingstonians was played the place went mad. To me this is a massive Skinhead record. The entertainment was regular battles between Spurs and Arsenal fans as the Royal was situated roughly between the two grounds. I used to buy records from Dykes and Dydens in West Green Road, Tottenham on a Saturday morning. I was usually the only white kid in there. I remember buying, "The Cooler" by The Wrigglers, a very rare tune on the Double D label for fifteen shillings, a lot of money for a single back then. To listen to top reggae tunes we used to go to a club in Dalston called The Four Aces. It was a black club but we never had any trouble. It had speakers like wardrobes.

I carried on buying records until the mid-'70s. After that I wasn't interested in reggae that went on about roots or going back to Ethiopia. Unfortunately, I lost some records at parties but I made sure I came away with compensation, a sheepskin or leather coat. Sheepskins. I love them. Tan coloured ones were the most popular but I managed to obtain a black one which I still have. Harrington jackets, superb. Beige coloured were the most popular. I also owned a Prince Of Wales check one. Sta-prest, most of us wore putty green ones worn with Ox Blood brogues or Doctor Martens. I've always worn Ox Blood shoes, still do. Shirts were Jaytex, Brutus or Ben Sherman's, checks and stripes. In fact my favourite shirt was a long-sleeved Ben Sherman in pale blue and white stripes which were very wide.I don't know if other Skinheads remember but this shirt had a lovely smell when it was ironed. I can't understand why there is a big argument nowadays over white Ben Shermans. (In *The Paint House Gang*, a 1972 study of Skinheads, one of the participants states that white Ben Shermans were never worn.) I had a long-sleeved Oxford weave, one which I got from Davis's in Tottenham which was a good Skinhead shop. Sleeveless V-necks and cardigans were also worn. I can remember a phase of wearing Levi cords (blue), crewneck blue jumper with the shirt collar out and brogues, probably late '69 or '70. I won't go into football violence – it's so fucking boring – but I reckon that London clubs had the smartest Skinheads in England by a long way. I know I keep saying that in different areas there were slightly different attitudes to clothes but I can't remember any of my mates wearing Levi's jean jackets. When they were worn with Levi jeans it looked a bit like Man at C&A.

We always thought it looked a bit Northern. Southend was an East London, Skinhead's Bank Holiday day out. The old bill used to hate us. Fuck off back to London etc. Hundreds of Skins running around, some scuffles, nothing serious. I must point out that not all Skinheads had a number one or number two haircut. Some had a very short college boy with a high parting, very similar to the hard Mods that appeared in 1965–66. Anyway, back to music. Many collectors nowadays are experts on reggae and rock steady but you must remember we were only kids so most parties that Skinheads went to jumped along to tunes like, "Long Shot Kick De Bucket", "John Jones", "Sufferer", "Nana," "Tighten Up", "Jackpot", "Vigaton 2" and "Fire Corner", etc etc. Big albums at the time were *Tighten Up Volume Two* and *No More*. Heartaches and most Trojan compilations whilst Pama, Gas, Amalgamated, Big Shot, Blue Cat, J.J., Duke and Unity and Upsetter were all big Skinhead labels. I can remember going up West one night, loads of Skinheads on a double decker bus, refusing to sit down. (Mind the suit mate.) All of a sudden the bus driver has pulled up outside Holborn nick, jumped out and gone into

THE SOUL STYLISTS

the police station for help. Loads of old bill pile on the bus and literally kicked us off. (I said mind the suit mate!)

I had a job driving a Transit pick-up truck for a steel company and I could use it after work and at weekends. One Saturday, driving towards Roman Road market with a truck full of mates, we were stopped by a traffic warden. I wound down the window and as I slowed down I knocked his cap off and drove off. Some of the boys were laughing so much they nearly fell out. I don't know how I got away with that one. I definitely wouldn't today. On the same day we wrecked a record shop in the market because they didn't have a decent reggae section. I think the end came round late '70, early '71 mainly because Skinheads had become a high street fashion. We started to grow our hair, get serious with girls and move on. I can remember Village Gate shops, topper shoes, and John Wesley Harding shirts coming along. But the fact is – the Skinhead always stays in your heart.'

Jim Cox – original Skinhead

* * *

The East End of London was an area made famous by the emergence of the publicity-hungry Kray twins whose dress sense mirrored the original Mod style. It is often cited as the birthplace of the Skinhead. If we take the Skinhead in another form, less smart than his Ivy League counterpart, now incorporating Cherry Red boots or Dr Martens, jeans with one-inch turn-ups, a Ben Sherman shirt, and a Harrington jacket into his wardrobe – plus the extreme cropped hair – this fact is probably correct. Again, it has much to do with the local area. Sheepskin coats, a Skinhead favourite, for example, were manufactured in the East End. The area also had a huge Mod presence. Its cloth factories have a great reputation for mohair. Many travelled from all over London to acquire suit material from the East End.

* * *

'I always thought it came from the East End. That's where I first saw it, probably at Upton Park when Coventry played them. And then it just evolved. There was no element of racism then. It was all fashion. Pure fashion.'

Gary Kingham – original Skinhead

'The whole scene was highly influenced by black culture – the haircut, the length of our trousers, the walk, the dances, some of the talk and, of course, the music, much of it was copied from the Rude Boy style. Black and white generally got on, we intermingled and if there was trouble it was usually about a woman.'

Nigel Mann

* * *

The *Daily Mirror* gave the movement its name on 3 September 1969. Not everyone was happy with the publicity. Reports came in of Skinheads being beaten up for talking to the press. Such intimidation didn't stop the publicity. Skinheads made great news. Violence, youth, violence – it's a magic formula that always makes for headlines. In fact, that summer, at the free Hyde Park gig given by the Rolling Stones, Skinheads made their first public appearance, announcing themselves to a rock culture now dominated by the hippy movement. The two movements swiftly became enemies. Many a 'hairy' was soon to feel the force of the young Skinhead's anger.

That this show of force was the first time that rock culture had been exposed to this new youth cult was not surprising, as the style had developed outside of it and become nationalised through the growth of football fans travelling in support of their teams.

* * *

'The first time I ever saw a Skinhead was when Chelsea came to play

Leicester in 1968. Tons of them showed up. I was absolutely fascinated by their dress, their style.'

Nigel Mann

'Absolutely, spot on. Chelsea versus Leicester just before Christmas '68 and Alan Birchenall scored the best goal of his life. That was the first time I saw Skinheads as well. They took the Leicester end. They were wearing mainly Levi's jeans. They were kind of Mod but a bit grubby looking. They had on donkey jackets and boots. Not Dr Marten boots but any kind of boots. Couldn't see the shirts because it was winter but they looked kind of East European, the drabbest crowd I had ever seen. Also, they didn't have short hair. It's become a myth that they all had short hair. They didn't. It was fairly short but with a bit on the side. There was a definite overlap between them and Mod.'

James Ferguson

'Within a week we all had our hair cropped and barbers had never been so busy. It's hard to convey just how different things were in the '60s and '70s. Fashions emanated from London and the further afield you lived the longer it took to reach you. In the very earliest stages The Look was pretty basic. Shirt jeans, Levi's or Wrangler and Wranglers faded were better but Levi's had that classic French seam that showed on the outside of your turn-ups.

The boots were originally ex-army issue, Cherry Reds and in the early days of the winter of '69, granddad vests and RAF greatcoats. But things moved on quickly.'

Nigel Mann

* * *

Outside of football, another element of their culure that was often emphasised was the Skinhead devotion to reggae music. (Indeed, many commentators have since wondered how Skinheads could love black music in such a strong fashion and yet harbour vicious racist tendencies. The fact of the matter is that the second-generation blacks quickly fought back against Skinheads. Unfortunately, it was the newly arrived Asians that bore the brunt of Skinhead violence.) Reggae was born in Jamaica, the result of a musical battle between Duke Reid and Coxsone Dodd. They ran competing sound systems, playing R&B records from the late '40s and early '50s at various dances. As the '50s came to an end, the supply of R&B records available on the island started to dry up thanks to the huge success of rock'n'roll.

To strengthen his position, Coxsone took some session musicians into a studio to record covers of the new R&B tunes. These records were then sold at dances and later to the public in general. No one knew it but the Jamaican recording industry had just taken its first tentative steps. As recording continued the musicians now began to play around with the tempo and rhythm of these tunes eventually arriving – through the work of pioneers such as Prince Buster – at a style they termed ska.

It soon found huge acclaim in England as did its successor, the rock steady sound in which the beat was slowed down and more emphasis put upon the rhythm section. Skinheads loved this new turn of events and just as the Mods lay claim to soul music through the work of labels such as Tamla and Atlantic, so the Skinheads fell in love with Trojan Records. This legendary label had emerged from a record mail order business set up by one Lee Gopthal, a Caribbean living in Neasden. In late 1963, he was approached by Island boss Chris Blackwell. Blackwell had a problem. Distribution of Island records was proving a real problem. Would Gopthal consider setting up a mail order business dealing in records? Gopthal agreed but soon found the business a hard one to enter. At one point he and his associates actually targeted black areas in London and sold their records door to door. By 1966, Gopthal had opened a few record shops including a famous stall in Shepherd's Bush market where many bought reggae records that remained unavailable in the usual outlets. In 1967,

THE SOUL STYLISTS

Gopthal moved into another area of the music business; licensing records from Jamaica. It was the smart move. The market was obviously buoyant but more importantly, it was expanding. In London at least, reggae was now ranking alongside R&B in terms of popularity. No wonder other Mods were now looking further afield – the Twisted Wheel in Manchester, for example – to fulfil their need for obscure soul.

Gopthal, aware of the capital's growing need for the music, responded by setting up various labels to release the work of selected Jamaican producers. For example, the Amalgamated label only released Joe Gibbs productions. In 1968, through sheer necessity, Gopthal and Blackwell found themselves sharing the same business address, 12 Neasden Lane, London, and the same line of work, licensing reggae tunes. To make sense of their dual ambitions, Gopthal proposed that he take over all of Blackwell's licensing labels and put them under one flagship label. This would then leave Blackwell free to concentrate on other matters. The name of the label would be Trojan which again takes us back to the very roots of the music. Duke Reid used a Trojan truck to transport his sound system. He was soon dubbed Duke Reid the Trojan. In honour of this, Island had set up the Trojan label to issue Reid's music but in reality it operated and died under the shadow of the more heavyweight Treasure Isle label. Gopthal and his contemporaries now revived Trojan and started business by licensing a succession of seven-inch singles. But Gopthal was not content with mere singles success such as Desmond Dekker's, '007 (Shanty Town)' a number 14 shot in 1967. He wanted more. He wanted to break into the lucrative album market, an area which reggae had spectacularly failed to make any impact in whatsoever. Thus, through extensive research into the problem, Gopthal discovered that West Indians felt albums were far too expensive and not varied enough. Which is when Gopthal launched his famed 'Tighten Up' series, featuring a collection of already released Trojan singles made by different artists and producers and retailing at a much lower price.

Between the late '60s and early '70s, these hugely popular compilations were packed with huge hits such as 'The Israelites' by Desmond Dekker, 'Liquidator' by Harry J.All Stars, 'Young Gifted and Black' by Bob Marcia, 'Long Shot Kick De Bucket' by The Pioneers and 'Double Barrel' by Dave and Ansell Collins.

* * *

'The music was unbelievable. A lot of the stuff you couldn't get in record shops unless it was a hit, which I could never figure out. So I used to go to Shepherd's Bush market for my reggae tunes and for soul there was a place in Rayner's Lane. I'll never forget that. Once I was with two black friends of mine and we were in this record shop. This old black woman worked there and she turned round to me and said, 'How come you don't go and listen to your Cliff Richard and leave us all alone?' I couldn't stop laughing.'

Terry Wheeler

* * *

Trojan enjoyed great chart success, all of their records helped to the top by thousands of Skinheads nationwide. The style had not been confined to London. The fashion had permeated faster and quicker than the Mod style because of the sudden growth of football crowds created in 1966 by England's victory at the World Cup. Thanks to Britain's improving infrastructure, fans could now travel to away games without much difficulty and therefore display new fashions. Many of the clothes were now easily available even if they were watered down versions. The Ben Sherman shirt, for example, gave its owner and designer riches beyond his dreams. Ben Sherman was a tailor who began manufacturing shirts from his factory in Hove in 1958. In 1963, he opened up his first eponymous shop next to the factory. It was at this point that he also added his name to one of his shirts.

THE SOUL STYLISTS

The Ben Sherman was a total copy of the American style. It had a button-down collar, was usually striped or simply plain coloured with a button at the back of the collar, a pleat running down the back, a hook at the top of that pleat and then two smaller pleats either side of the back. Ben Sherman's life was transformed by this shirt. The success of the shirt established the foundations for the huge business it attracts today and it drove its creator towards a life filled with women, gambling and alcohol.

Its main competitor for the Skinheads' affections was the collarless union shirt which came in plain colours or stripes and later on Brutus – who did create the best tartan styles or the much derided Jaytex shirt. Fred Perry shirts – three-buttoned with piping on the collar and short sleeves were popular.

By 1968, Harrington jackets were also available in Britain as were Dr Martens, Levi Sta-prest and 501 jeans, Crombie coats, sheepskins, trilby hats and braces. The new styles were, as usual, dictated by the normal few Faces but with a crucial difference. Where the Mods had sought to express themselves through their style and taste, mass Skinhead clothing was purpose led; would any item of clothing be a hindrance in a street battle? It was an important point. Clashes between opposing fans at football grounds had soon became commonplace, much of it caused by Skinhead activity. The fact of the matter is that, by and large, the young Skinheads had gained a reputation for hate. They despised just about everyone. They hated students, they hated hippies and 'hairies', they hated bikers, they hated Asians, anyone in fact who wasn't one of them. Their appearance was designed to ignite fear not inspiration. But fashion was changing. Lines were becoming more loose. The popularity of long hair signified a shift away from masculine codes. John Simon noted it.

After the success of the Ivy Shop, he and his partner now opened up another shop, the Squire shop in Brewer Street, London. An ex-butcher's shop, John and an employee, Stuart Molloy redesigned the shop. They scrubbed clean the big wooden butcher's tables and stood them in the middle of the shop with shoes and shirts placed on them. There were cubby-holes everywhere, filled with American clothing goods.

* * *

'No one part of that shop was inaccessible to anyone – customers or people who worked there. Again, we used that New England look. Wooden floor, dark woods, that kind of thing and we also had no counter which was the same as the Ivy Shop.'

John Simon

* * *

For many, the Squire shop was a completely new shopping experience. But trouble was brewing between Simon and his partner. Kwintner wanted to expand, as quickly as possible, and Simon feared a dilution of his vision. The ground was set and in the early '70s the two parted company.

* * *

'John was the purist and Jeff the businessman. I worked for them and I think relations got really strained. So John kept the Ivy Shop and maybe Squire and Jeff took over the others.'

Stuart Molloy – head of Jones, Covent Garden

'I remember five rows of us went to see this film called *Bronco Bullfrog*. The opening sequence a guy comes out and he's wearing a penny round collar and a floral shirt. Everyone just bursts out laughing. But four weeks later we've all got the kit on. I remember buying a shirt and tie set with a round collar and I threw the tie away and wore the shirt. Things just evolved. Obviously, the hair grew longer and we went into the Suedehead thing.'

Gary Kingham

Before, when he walked the street, he and his friends were apart, separate and very noticeable. Now there were thousands of Skinheads roaming the towns and the papers carried reports on them every day. Skinheads were overground and public. Like all such movements which were created away from the spotlight the glare of publicity was lethal. To ward off its impending doom, the Skinhead now entered a process of change. At first this revolved around a growing out of the hair and a smartening up of his look. This smarter version was named the Suedehead, a title derived from his cropped hair growing out and thus giving the appearance and texture of suede. Many of the clothes remained the same although Suedeheads were never fond of Dr Martens or braces. They much preferred Royals brogues or loafers such as Frank Wright's or Kingwsay. They liked suits made of Tonik material (made by Dormeuil), Crombies (some of whom used the top pocket to display their football colours through the use of various coloured handkerchiefs) Ben Sherman or maybe Brutus shirts, Levi Sta-prest, coloured socks, etc.

* * *

'It was really a passing fashion. As I remember it, it was just a style that Mods and Skinheads went through. They were semi-smart Skins. They'd wear 501s but with a smart jacket and brogues or loafers. The jeans thing was dead serious. You did buy them and sit in the bath and get out the vim to get them faded and wearable because they were made of big heavy industrial material. But the Suedehead thing was dead by about 1973.'

Ady Croasdell – DJ at 6T's club

* * *

In between this look there then briefly emerged the Smoothies. The Smoothies pitched themselves somewhere between the Suedehead and the Skinhead – casual but cool with their tank tops and round-collared shirts. But in truth it was all just a variation on a theme, that theme being young British working-class kids at the start of the '60s adopting an American look and spinning out their teenage years to the sound of soul and reggae. By the end of 1973, it was basically all over. Never again would The Look dominate street fashion to such an extent. The streets of Britain would not be witness to gangs of kids in button-down shirts, smart trousers, smart shoes, brimming with style and attitude. The winds of change were picking up speed.

* * *

'When the hairy thing really got heavily underway that undermined the whole shop. The shop went on but there was no big steam on it. We ticked over, put it like that.'

John Simon

'All good things come to an end and we knew it when a well-respected lad called Willy turned up at the Il Rondo club in Leicester one Wednesday night wearing sandals and his sheepskin coat turned inside out.'

Nigel Mann

'George Melly wrote a book called *Revolt Into Style*. First he had a go at Mods, saying they were nasty little tykes. Then he had a go at Skinheads saying they were all C-stream drop-out dumbos. No. Wrong. We were everything. I went to grammar school and I was fine. Lots of others were as well. He was judging it on pure prejudice and that happened a lot. It happens because nine times out of ten it's written about by middle-class people who have never been through this kind of thing. For me it felt great. You're amongst your own kind with the music and the clothes. I loved it. So when I read these things about fascism, it's been stolen, they've stolen something that meant so much to me.'

James Ferguson

CHAPTER FOUR

BRUT, SWEAT AND TEARS

YOU WALKED DOWN THE STAIRS, turned back on yourself and you were confronted by a warren of rooms. In one of them, Roger Eagle was playing a tough R&B selection and that sent you pushing through the crowd and into the room where he stood deejaying in a cage built from welded bicycle wheels, hence the club's name. The asphalt floor beneath you was desperately sticky and a lot of the girls had already changed into their ballet shoes. Some of the guys were wearing black leather gloves because there was condensation dripping off the black painted walls, running down in small rivers and soaking into the floor. But that didn't matter. Those were just mere details because here, in the Twisted Wheel in 1967, there was an atmosphere so warm, so friendly, so right that you just hoped the speed would soon kick in and then you could throw yourself headfirst into the night.

* * *

'The Twisted Wheel was a dump, an absolute bloody dump. Roger Eagle told me, and his exact words were, "Dave, it was run on the old New York philosophy, don't fix it if it ain't broken." It was an unsanitary bloody place really. But it had the most wonderful atmosphere.'

Dave Clegg – original soul fan

In the '60s, fashions didn't travel fast. They took their time to permeate throughout the rest of the country. Modernism was no different. It may have started in London in the very early '60s but up North, where London was viewed with huge mistrust, it took its time to spread. The media coverage of the seaside battles in 1964 and a national pop show like *Ready Steady Go* did much to publicise one aspect of Modernism, but as we have seen this was very much at the end of its original ideals.

In London, Modernism had died, replaced by the Kings Road set and the advent of the hippies and so the North now became the standard bearer. In many Northern counties, a second generation of Mods soon established their presence. From them came the enduring Northern Soul scene which thrives to this day.

* * *

'What you have to realise is that travel was impossible. There was no M62 connecting Yorkshire and Lancashire and because we were young we didn't drive. So London was the other side of the world. So we didn't care about what London was doing. That first lot of Mods hardly touched us.'

Dave Clegg

'The coolest kid in my school was a guy called Pod. He was an out and out Mod. He had a tailored jacket instead of a school blazer. He always went out with dolly birds and he had a Lambretta GP 200. So at the age of 12, looking at people like Pod with his scooter and knowing that he was probably getting shagged every night and he looked so great, you just thought that's what I want to have – girls, clothes, scooters and music.'

Ian Dewhurst – Wigan Casino DJ

* * *

In 1965, Tamla Motown Records was finally launched in the UK. Within a year, its acts – The Four Tops, Marvin Gaye, The Supremes, Stevie Wonder, Smokey Robinson, et al. – were ruling. Motown was unstoppable. Hit after hit. But they were not the only ones to find fertile ground in Britain. Atlantic Records was also making inroads into the British consciousness and dividing people over the merits of its grittier soul sound (especially that propagated by one of its main licensees, the famed Stax label) in comparison to Motown's pop–soul sensibility. Through such labels, soul music could now launch a major assault on the British charts and in response to this invasion, various soul clubs, north of Watford, appeared everywhere, playing a music that London was now tending to ignore in favour of either psychedelia or the emerging funk sound of artists such as James Brown.

* * *

'The first record I bought was "I Feel Love" by Felice Taylor. I think that was about 1967 so I would have been twelve. I remember that for the next three years at school two distinct camps emerged. There was the progressive camp who had, "In Search Of The Lost Chord" by the Moody Blues, Cream and all that stuff. And then there were the ones that used to go to the youth clubs where all they played was Motown. All the youth clubs did that, they played just soul. By the time I got to fifteen I was well and truly on that Motown thing. I was actively going back and buying things that I missed.'

Ian Dewhurst

'I'm fifteen years old and there is a club in Huddersfield called the Tahiti Two. That was the one your father said, "You don't go there." That was the club that had the old knock once, ring the bell and the panel in the door opened and the guy looked at you. I had been going to a coffee bar called Studio 58 which was for Mods and I got friendly with these guys that were two years older than me. They've got the mohair suits. They've got the scooters. And they took me down the Tahiti Two on a Friday night. I walked in and I was absolutely knocked out. I've got on my best jacket that my mother had bought me and I am thinking I am the dog's bollocks. I looked round at these guys with their suits on and all these women and my mouth fell open. And the music. It was on a free jukebox and it was all Stax, Atlantic and Motown. It was magic.'

Dave Clegg

* * *

As we have seen, one of the first clubs to make a name for itself in the North was the Twisted Wheel in Manchester which opened in 1963 in Brazennose Street before moving to Whitworth Street in 1965. Its doors stayed open until the last Saturday of January 1971 and its musical direction was created by the late Roger Eagle whose selection of quality R&B of all tempos won him many admirers.

* * *

'The Rolling Stones used to go to the Wheel after a gig in Manchester and there is a story that when they walked in Roger played all of their first album by the original artists in track order. His musical policy was simple. If it was good you played it and at this time it was records that were on British release. It was only about 1969 or '70 that you started getting records on import like "Agent Double O Soul" by Edwin Starr or Leon Haywood's "Baby Reconsider". Now people can go on about a musical policy but if a DJ plays a record and the crowd don't like it then it ain't gonna get played. The records that were played had to be accepted by the crowd and they had to be good enough to displace something that was on his playlist, because the turnover wasn't that great, it really wasn't.'

Dave Clegg

In a very short time, the Twisted Wheel had established itself as a major UK soul club. It was made up of a series of rooms, small and dank, and live acts were often presented to a packed club. It is said that when the hugely loved and respected Junior Walker and the All Stars played the Wheel, he had to be passed over the crowd's head so as to make an exit.

* * *

'I only ever saw that room upstairs full once and that's when Junior Walker was on and they piped his set throughout the whole club. That was the most expensive night in the Wheel as well. It was normally ten shillings and sixpence with no act on, fifteen shillings with an act on or one pound for someone really special. But it was thirty shillings for Junior Walker.'

Dave Clegg

* * *

The Wheel's reputation as a major Mod club spread all over Britain. Even a handful of dedicated London Mods, starved of soul music in the capital, would make the weekly trip to Manchester, displaying the latest London look. But the club's reputation also carried a slight edge.

* * *

'I have got no photographs from inside the Wheel and I doubt if anyone has because you wouldn't dare take in a camera. You wouldn't dare wear a watch, they'd rob you for it. Lots of guys used to come in from another club, the Blue Note, at five in the morning and they'd wait near the back door. When the Wheel ended you didn't go out the front, you went out the back door into a back alley and then up onto the main street so there were one or two, let's say, who would take advantage and you had to be careful.

Usually you were okay because there were loads of regulars you would meet up with. We used to catch the train from Huddersfield, used to be one at nine, got you in at quarter to ten, thirteen shillings and sixpence return. You'd meet people outside the Dolphin coffee bar or meet the guys from Wales on Victoria Street Station and that's where you'd score. Dexys were ten a quid but you'd turn them down 'cos you knew you could get green and clears at the same price. I did one all-nighter straight and I've never done it since because it just wasn't the same. You weren't in the same frame of mind as everybody else.'

Dave Clegg

* * *

Naturally, dancing was an essential component of the Twisted Wheel experience. At the time, it was usual for guys and girls to form a circle and shuffle to the rhythm. Somebody would then step into the centre, express themselves and then move out and the next person would take over. This was common practice in most clubs. In the Lantern in Market Harborough, for example, people danced the Moonhop. Again a circle was formed but instead of shuffling people would clap hands and jump up and down using alternate legs. Someone would then enter the circle and perform. It is likely that the dances that were executed within the circle displayed the flamboyance that would later characterise Northern Soul dancing with its back flips, twists and spins.

* * *

'If you had Dr Martens on you couldn't dance sideways because they were too sturdy. That's how the Moonhop came to be because everyone was wearing Dr Martens so you had to go up and down. Then you'd go into the circle and do your bit. In the Mod scene there was a different dance every week so in the late '60s dances were always evolving. In the early '70s they hit upon the style which was perfect for the music. For the Mods it was that Stax/Atlantic music, more jerky stuff, but once it got into that solid, non-stop fast Tamla beat, people developed their own dances,'

Ady Croasdell

* * *

Although there are some who deny it, purely for reasons of image and because of their wariness over media perversion of their culture, one of the scene's undeniable forces was the use of drugs, amphetamines. Which is why it wasn't too long before the police became very interested in Britain's all-night soul scene. In 1971, the Twisted Wheel's application for a new licence was refused. Four years previously, Roger Eagle had quit due to his dislike for Motown music and the parsimony of the club's owners.

* * *

'The City Council didn't want any all-night dances within the city of Manchester. All night dances mean drugs. However, it wasn't due to a police objection. I firmly believe to this day that the police wanted it open because they could keep their eye on everybody that was into amphetamines and breaking into chemists. I stopped going in November of 1970 because I saw fighting there. It was getting rough. One guy came out of the back door and somebody fancied his shoes and took them off him. These guys were intimidating and it didn't help that we were all speeding and we were young. After the Wheel closed several all-nighters opened up in Yorkshire.

We had the Metro in Wakefield, we had Ernie's in Leeds and just before The Wheel closed there was Harrison's Hoist in Earby. All of them got raided. Open for three weeks and then the police came in, pulled everybody out, even took urine samples for internal possession of drugs. There were no all-nighters to go to. Closed them all down, especially in West Yorkshire. Getting an all-night licence in those days was very difficult.'

Dave Clegg

THE SOUL STYLISTS

111

'What wrecked the Twisted Wheel was the kids demanding faster music. Eventually, Roger felt that he was being restricted because the crowd were so demanding of having the fast ones, presumably because they had all this speed pumping through them. That pissed him off and eventually a new breed of DJ came through focusing on the more up tempo stuff which in turn became the dominant sound.'

Ian Dewhurst

'In Roger's words, he didn't like the pill-heads that were changing the music.'

Dave Clegg

* * *

In his last ever interview, granted to the fanzine *The New Breed* in 1999, Eagle explained that he was never a 'high profile DJ'. Instead, he concentrated on the music, playing up to six or seven hours in a night. His playlist would include artists like Ray Charles, James Brown, Fats Domino, Bo Diddley, Booker T and the MGs, John Lee Hooker, The Mar-Keys, Muddy Waters, The Drifters, Big Joe Turner, Bill Black's Combo, Solomon Burke. Eagle recalled stirring up a healthy relationship with Guy Stevens, these two influential DJs exchanging records and respect. He explained that his departure from the Wheel – two years at its original home in Brazennose Street and one year at Whitworth Street – was caused by the club's owners, the Abadi brothers, refusing him a wage rise and by the changes chemical abuse wrought in his audience. 'Kids were in trouble with the pills and all they wanted was that kind of fast tempo soul dance,' he recalled. There was a sadness in his voice.

* * *

'At the same time as the Wheel there was also a scene taking place in Northampton and Bedfordshire. We'd hang around the people from Northampton and Kettering and Corby. All of them had very good clubs. You'd hear about dancers through the grapevine and you'd go down there to check them out. There was a South Midlands and a north Home Counties scene that went down as far as Luton and developed on its own while the Wheel was going on. I never went to the Twisted Wheel but I didn't need to because there were great local things going on.

The DJs in the clubs probably did follow the Wheel's lead but when people say Northern Soul started at the Wheel, well, it didn't. It started in other places at the same time. That said, the Wheel was probably the best. I remember when they came down to the Lantern in Market Harborough when the Wheel had closed. They were so well dressed. We were smart-casual but they were smart-smart. They had the blazer badges, proper gold crests on their top pockets.'

Ady Croasdell

'They wore one black leather glove each and they were miles ahead of us. We were into "Boy From New York City" by the Ad Libs but they were into "Nothing Worse Than Being Alone" by the same group but a much classier record. When they came to the Lantern there was a bit of tension but I said to my mate, "We should embrace them. They're taking us to another level." And they did.'

Brian Taylor – businessman

'For me, growing up as a late '60s Mod the ultimate cool for me was the early '60s Mods dancing to Major Lance and all those mid-tempo beautifully crafted songs. It was much later that the music speeded up.'

Ady Croasdell

* * *

In 1970, surveying these soul developments, the writer Dave Godin penned two articles about soul in the North for the magazine, *Blues and Soul*. He used the term 'Northern Soul' and it was quickly adapted. At first, the fashion was classic Modernist but as the years passed the clothes – as all levels of fashion did throughout the first part of the '70s – lost their strict lines and tightness. Trousers in particular ballooned out, with one style, Oxford bags, gaining much popularity.

* * *

'They saved my life, Oxford bags. I got pulled into Notting Hill police station once. I'd just bought an ounce of gear. The Flying Squad stopped me. I knew they'd been following me when I left this dealer's house so I had put the gear down my pants. They took me to the desk and said, empty your pockets. As I stood there the bag slid right down my trousers but because they were bags, the trousers covered it. I stood on it and as the copper went through my wallet I was able to kick it under the radiator. Okay, I lost £200 but those bags saved my life.'

Brian Taylor

'In the early days of the scene, I wore a wool worsted bottle green suit. It had three buttons up the front, four buttons on the cuff, slanted pockets, two-inch flap, ticket pocket, pocket on the inside for cigarettes, single vent eighteen inches at the back and flared from the waist. Trousers, fourteen inch bottoms. I wore desert boots during the day but at night it was Church's Oxford shoes or brogues. Now your Levi's had to be faded with a patch from the back pocket of an old pair put on your knee. And you would wear a Ben Sherman shirt. Dave Godin once visited the Twisted Wheel and he wrote, "Never have I seen so many Ben Shermans gathered in one place."'

Dave Clegg

'Every week I'd buy a Ben Sherman not a Brutus. The difference was that a red Brutus would have white buttons but a red Ben Sherman would have red buttons. I'd been at an all-nighter, dancing all night. In the morning we'd all go to the Blue Boar service station on the M1. Because you'd been dancing, you'd all be hot and sticky so you'd go to the bogs, have a wash, change your clothes. In the bogs, I'd hung this brand new red Ben Sherman shirt up to wear. I started washing but when I turned around it was gone. Instead, there was this stinky old Brutus hanging there. So I grabbed it, went into the café upstairs and I see this guy – who has never spoken to me in his life – sat there wearing my brand new shirt talking to a girl called Sue Bushby. I go up to him, I say, "You're wearing my brand new shirt" and he gets up and he whispers to me, "Sorry mate but I'm trying to get off with this bird and I thought the shirt might sway it." That was Pasquale and we've been best friends ever since.'

Brian Taylor

'I had this red checked Arnold Palmer shirt which I used to wear at all-nighters and people used to come and offer me money for it. It was a thirty-bob shirt and people would offer me a fiver for it. Then I went to university and made friends with this Skinhead/Suedehead guy. We always used to wear the button-down shirts but one term I came back with a shirt that had a rounded collar. The guy was devastated. He didn't talk to me for a week.'

Ady Croasdell

* * *

The outside world – as in all things Mod – was at best a distraction and at worse an irritant as an increasing police interference began to threaten the Soul Stylist's way of life. Worse than that, the success of Motown irked those who wanted to keep their scene private. They were snobs and they were purists and many were determined to protect their midnight undergrounds from unwelcome intruders who might know the hit records but had not one inkling of the codes and rituals involved. The in crowd now started demanding rarer sounds. They didn't want to hear the soul hits that were being played on Radio One (launched in 1967) or national television; too popular, too obvious. They wanted everything exclusive and they wanted a great time to go with it. That meant ingesting amphetamines to dance out the all-nighter.

* * *

'There was an ethic which said that if you get these people in who all week have been doing sluggish jobs, ten to twelve hours a day, when they eventually go out on the weekend they don't fuck around. They want to dance all night and get as high as kites. They wanted to pack as much fun as they could in.'

Ian Dewhurst

'Personally, I don't want to talk about it. Some of it was part of the scene and it happened and I can only remember three people I know who never did it – and two of them were my mum and dad – but no, I don't want to talk about it.'

Gilly – original soul fan

'If there hadn't been amphetamines there wouldn't have been all-nighters.'

Ady Croasdell

'If anyone didn't take drugs, basically they were the exception. I remember Black Val from Manchester; she was renowned because she didn't take them. To be honest, I don't know which was the most important, whether they took drugs to listen to the music or they liked the music and needed the drugs. Once speed got hard to get hold of they would take anything and quite a few died from barbiturate overdosing or being killed driving home on a Sunday morning. It was a drugs scene at first. You can go to an all-nighter now and no one will mention drugs whereas in the past, first question, what have you had?'

Brian Taylor

'The Bradford blokes were notorious for doing chemists. They would plan their route to the all-nighter which would always be via a chemist which was thirty miles out of the way.'

Ian Dewhurst

'I would go to the library mid-week and get out a big map of Norfolk. Then I'd get the pharmaceutical register which has all the chemists and I would make a list. Then I'd get the map and draw out a route. On the day, we would drive past a chemist, might be alarmed – a lot of shops weren't in those days – so forget it, drive on to the next one. By the end of the day we'd say the best one is so and so, let's go and do that. I can remember doing one in Norfolk and coming out of the front door as the milkman was putting the milk on the doorstep. "Morning!" I said. Another one I did, I took the pharmacist's coat off the back of the door and put it on. I was stood there emptying the till. Suddenly there was a knock on the door and there's an old woman waving her prescription at me and I'm going, "Sorry love, can't help you, come back tomorrow morning."'

Brian Taylor

'I remember these Skinheads who were into the scene, they had five cans of Dexys with 1,000 pills in them and they hid them in this field. But one of the guys who hid his can was off his head and he couldn't remember where he had hidden it. So the next morning, in a field in the middle of nowhere, there must have been about sixty Skinheads piling through the hedges and searching. Even to this day I go past that field and I wonder…'

Ady Croasdell

'A good pharmacy had everything stored alphabetically. So you would go to D because most of them began with D – Dexedrine, Drynamil, Durophet – then you'd go to the till for a bit of cash. But in 1974 I was doing a chemist in Wales and there was a big white cabinet on the wall, took about two hours to open and inside there was a letter from the Home Office saying that all pharmacists must have security cabinets. What that meant was that once you spent time opening that cabinet you took the lot. You had to take everything whereas before I'd just taken the speed. Often, I took the whole cabinet. The cabinet would have a spotlight on it so the police driving by could pull up and see it. So you didn't have time to open it, you'd just rip it off and take it away with you. That meant we also took class "A" drugs and all that would go to this one guy while we took the speed. I only found out later that all the cocaine from these chemists was keeping a well-known entertainer going throughout the '70s.'

Brian Taylor

'The difference now is that the drugs then were made by pharmacists and were, therefore, a lot less harmful than today where you've got guys making drugs and feeding people all kinds of shit.'

Dave Prest – original soul fan

'I met a girl at Cleethorpes. For our first date I took her along to hi-jack a van making deliveries at a chemist's shop. Mary Chapman ran Cleethorpes. During the all-nighter she would tell my girlfriend that the squad had been asking for me at the door. She would later write to me when I was inside.'

Brian Taylor

'That's when I first discovered the Northern Soul crowd were an extension of the Mod ethic, only they were more underground and a bit more fanatical about their music. I went to a do in Hedmuntile in Yorkshire.

There were seven lads there with custom-made blazers, all with Torch logos on them. I got talking to them and they told me about this all-nighter called The Torch in Stoke-on-Trent. But what I noticed the most is that they all carried themselves a little bit differently. They were all slightly disdainful that the DJ was only playing Motown. They had that attitude about them.'

Ian Dewhurst

* * *

Again, Motown can be seen as another major step within the scene's development. Its huge success in the States meant that hundreds of soul entrepreneurs all started their own tiny labels, driven in the hope of repeating Motown owner Berry Gordy's amazing success. The result was a series of small record companies – Carnival, Topper and many others – that issued records by unknown but talented artists, many of whom were doomed to obscurity in their homeland but who would eventually find true recognition on the Northern scene. Artists such as Tommy Hunt, The Flirtations, Maxine Brown, Little Ann, Bobby Parris, Major Lance, and many others, finally received due acclaim thanks to the devotees of Northern Soul. The record companies also acquired followers as many soul devotees began acquiring whole catalogues of obscure labels such as Shrine or Artic, records that never even gained national release in America. Northern Soul fans treated these labels and artists with huge affection and love. Which was only right. It was their records which laid the foundations for this fascinating scene in the first place.

* * *

'The prototype rhythm for Northern Soul is "I Can't Help Myself" by the Four Tops. That's what a lot of the records are based on.'

Ady Croasdell

'I was really lucky. Bradford market had a record stall called Bostocks. They had thousands of imports because they had just bought the MGM/Verve warehouse in Philadelphia and they had stalls all over the North banging out these singles. They used to sell them, twenty for a quid. I think I earned £2.50 in those days so I used to go up to Bostocks every Saturday lunchtime and buy forty records. There would be a lot of bollocks in there but there would always be some killers.

"You Hit Me Where It Hurts" by Alice Clark, "What Would I Do" by The Tymes, "Thumb A Ride" by Earl Wright, which at the time – I didn't know this – there were only three copies in the country and that is a legendary record. Anyway, over the space of two years I probably accumulated maybe a thousand 45s and then I started deejaying at Leeds Central.'

Ian Dewhurst

'In Leicester market Jeff King ran a record stall. He did the first ever bootleg. It was "She Blew A Good Thing" by the American Poets and it was the first Northern Soul bootleg in this country. I went to his stall and he had stacks of them The records were on a label I hadn't heard of but I bought a few. Jeff had a friend called Batman. He would come up and ask if you wanted anything. Then you'd walk off with him and he would open his blazer and there would be a pile of pills inside. Black bombers, ten a quid, Dexys at twenty a quid.'

Ady Croasdell

'Out of all of them I think Alan Day was my favourite DJ. Alan worked in Selectadisc but he was one of us. Nowadays there is this division between the crowd and the DJ but back then there was none of that. He was just really into it. If he played a record that no one danced to, he would take it off and he'd whiz it across the dance floor like a frisbee. He played in a booth and sometimes you'd see him trying to get down the stairs, falling all over the place. As I said, he was one of us, not like some of the guys you get today. He was a real blockers DJ. One night I told him I'd had ten black bombers. He said, so what? He'd had thirty. And he had.'

Brian Taylor

'When I was thirteen, one of my greatest heros, certainly my first hero as a DJ, was a guy called Alan Day. He used to live in Burton on Trent. And he was a big name at Up The Junction and particularly at The Torch. He was one hell of a character. He's got some record outlets up and around Wakefield and also in the Yorkshire area but he used to have a shop in New Street, Burton on Trent, called the House of Sound and he was way ahead of most people. He had such a vast stock of imports. One of the first people in this country to have them. Before, everybody used to be mucking around with British releases and that. And suddenly there was this guy Alan Day and he's got this enormous stock of imports. I remember I used to go in. I was a very, very naïve kid and I went into his shop in Burton buying records off him and he'd be stood behind the counter and he'd be absolutely off his head, this was ten o'clock in the morning but he was a great inventor, for the usage of imports anyway.'

Gilly

* * *

One of the earliest striking features of the scene was the prices that these hard-to-get singles started to command. Northern Soul singles have always erred on the expensive side. They're hard to locate and have to be imported into the country as many are never given a British release. Because the initial pressing of such records tended to be quite low, as the company in question survived on low funds, many singles have an exclusivity denied their counterparts in other areas of music. Today one seven-inch record, such as Frank Wilson's 'Do I Love You' (500 singles were pressed as promo copies and then withdrawn under Wilson's own insistence) is worth thousands and thousands of pounds.

* * *

'In the early days you paid a fiver. If you paid a tenner for a record that would be a severe chunk. My first wage was £22 a week so that gives you a clue. As the years went by and the scene got more popular the prices, I think, got out of control.'

Ian Dewhurst

* * *

The Northern scene created a new breed of record dealer. At clubs, most notably the famed Wigan Casino, the promoters would allow the dealers to set up stalls where they could sell their singles. Many of them quickly forged links with the DJs who were always hungry for exclusive tunes. The art of covering up labels soon became widespread amongst DJs. A dealer would sell a DJ a one off copy of a record. The DJ would then cover up the label and also change the title and artist so making it nigh on impossible for anyone else to either recognise or secure the same copy. That meant that soul fans who wanted to hear certain records were now obliged to follow certain DJs. It was a practice that had been standard for years amongst sound system DJs in Jamaica.

* * *

'At the time, Ian Levene was the number one for discovering records. His dad owned a casino in Blackpool so Levene was able to go to the States three times a year and come back with all these great tunes. He played at the Highland Room at the Blackpool Mecca with Colin Curtis and that became the place for the die hards. In 1973, the main dealers were people like Julian Bentley, Brian "45" Phillips, John Anderson and this guy called Simon Soussan. Soussan was a tailor in Burtons in Leeds. The story goes that he used to hang around the Persian–Arabic crowd in a club called Madisons. One day, he walked into Jumbo Records in Leeds, which was the only shop at the time to sell soul records, and the music hit him. He actually had a revelation. The guy dived headfirst into it and he amassed a serious amount of records.

After about eighteen months, he decided to base himself in the States and dedicate his life to music and record dealing. I used to go to the States commercially as well and he was the guy I dealt with although whether he really had got the rights to many of the records he licensed I couldn't really say.'

Ian Dewhurst

* * *

The next club to gain a big reputation was The Torch in Stoke.

* * *

'It used to be once a month and then Up The Junction in Crewe opened so there would be an all-nighter every two weeks. Anne and I went to The Torch five or six times, usually when there was somebody live on like Major Lance or Fontella Bass. I don't think I ever left the balcony. It was a big old cinema, just one big room. You've got a balcony with a bar and the popular drink at the time was brown ale and coke shandies. So you've got the balcony, you've got two stairs either side and the balcony overlooked the stage.

That's when people stopped dancing in circles, they were just dancing as a mass on the floor and it was all a crush. Now before, we never knew who was deejaying unless they were friends of ours. You didn't give a shit who was deejaying. But at The Torch you started getting the DJs on stage and they got above their station. They were no longer in contact with the audience. Then you start getting the names appearing on posters and that's continued to this day. And as much as I love the music not one of those guys could play for four hours.'

Dave Clegg

'This guy Pete Tilsey, he was on the balcony at The Torch and a record came on and he leapt off the balcony and broke both his wrists.'

Brian Taylor

'I was pretty dammed annoyed that I never went to The Torch. When I was at school there was a guy who was older than me and I used to see him through the windows on a Monday and he would be fast asleep in lessons and I'd think, yeah, I know where you've been this weekend. It was actually three guys out of my village who used to go. They were all big names. Pretty tasty guys. But my mum wouldn't let me go. Simple as that.'

Gilly

* * *

If there was one characteristic of the scene it was the relationship between audience and DJ. At the outset the two were indistinguishable from one another. Fans of the music to a man (and girl), it was not in the slightest bit unusual for someone to approach the DJ with a record they had just secured and ask for a play of it.

* * *

'You would be playing the records – I don't say you DJ, you play the records to the people – because this music is for sharing. If you were playing records I'd walk in and give you one of mine. Here you are, play this record and you knew it would be safe.'

Dave Clegg

'We were guilty of being snobbish. I remember Kegsy was this nutter from Bradford, the sort of guy who would set off on a Friday night with twenty pence and a Mars bar in his pocket and would come home on Sunday night with fifty quid. I can remember Kegsy coming to the Central with a Dean Parrish record in his hand. It was on Laurie and the Laurie label looked like shit. It looked like the sort of thing you would find at any market that's selling imports. He came up to me and he said, "Play this, it's a killa." Now this is only the Central in Leeds, it's not going to kill me to play it. Nonetheless, I put it on the headphones and it starts with this horrible guitar. I said, "No, you must be fucking mad." So off he went. I think he went to Richard Searling at Va Va's which was a brilliant club in Bolton and he wouldn't play it. Then he went to Blackpool on the Saturday and Levine and Curtis wouldn't play it. Everyone's saying, "Dean Parrish on Laurie – fucking pop record." He finally cracked it at seven in the morning at Wigan with Russ Winstanley. Russ to his credit played it and from that one play it became the record everyone had to have. And of course that record closed Wigan every Saturday night.

Some records you had to champion. For example, I was the first person to have Tobi Legend's "Time Will Pass You By" but it took two years for that record to take off. At one point I didn't dare play it. It was a record that was guaranteed to clear the floor. But then you'd get these aficionados who would demand, "Play that record again". So it would end up as a record you would play for them. You couldn't play it in the middle of the night. You would have to wait until the early hours and build it from there. In the end, those two records plus Jimmy Radcliffe's "Long After Tonight Is All Over" became famous as the three records that closed Wigan every Saturday night.'

Ian Dewhurst

'Wrong. Before "I'm On My Way" had turned up, Dean Parrish had also hit big on the scene with "Tell Her." So there were plenty of reasons for Levene and Co. to take a good look at this record.

The truth is the record – "I'm On My Way" – had been discovered and played at an all-nighter two years prior to Wigan and this is the story. In late '71, maybe early '72, a few of the Northern faces moved to the Kettering area because there was more gear and better all-nighters. A number of them were staying in a house with a local DJ and record dealer called Glen Bellamy. One Saturday morning, Swish, a well known face from York turned up at Glen's house. Swish wants to know where the nearest bookies and second-hand record shop are. Glen drops him off at the bookies and also points out the record shop but he tells Swish there is nothing there as he has already trawled it many times himself. That evening Swish arrives back at the house skint (horse fell) but with three singles. Glen plays the records and takes a fancy to one. He offers to buy the record from Swish but Swish says he'll keep hold of it for a bit. That same night, Glen DJ'ed at the Bletsoe all-nighter in Bedford and played that record for the very first time. It was Dean Parrish's "I'm On My Way" and the rest is history.'

Brian Taylor

'By the time The Torch closed, the shirt collars had all changed. They were now rounded and everyone's hair was a bit longer, a bit wavier. Nobody stayed Skinhead or Mod, they went with it. It was the transition between Mod and Wigan. By the time Wigan Casino started in 1973, the trousers had been getting baggier and baggier and one of the reasons was because people were now spinning on the dance floor and these trousers made the spinning look good. I went to one of the very first all-nighters at Wigan and it was just another all-nighter.'

Ady Croasdell

'Prior to Wigan, if one new person turned up at an all-nighter you said, "Who's that new person?" After Wigan that never happened.'

Brian Taylor

* * *

Soul at Wigan Casino was started by a DJ named Russ Winstanley. He had previously deejayed around Wigan but when he heard The Torch was closing he moved swiftly to provide an alternative all-nighter. Situated in Station Road, the Casino was basically a run-down ballroom with a balcony on the first floor. It was managed by one Gerry Marshall. Reluctant at first to accede to Winstanley's approach, harsh economics soon swayed Marshall. On the first night they attracted a crowd of over 600 people. Within a year it would be one of the most famous clubs in Britain. It would take Northern Soul to new heights of popularity and in the process wound it so badly that it would take years for it to recover.

* * *

'It was the right club at the right time. Definitely. The Torch had closed and there were no Saturday all-nighters so it could hardly fail. It had a massive captive audience. I went there on the first night and I didn't get there until three in the morning and already there was a great atmosphere. In the downstairs bar it was like a mecca for collectors. They had come from everywhere, Liverpool, Wales, Carlisle. They had all turned out. See, Blackpool shut at two in the morning so you had to get there by at least ten at night to get your four hours in. But because Wigan was all night they far preferred to go there.'

Ian Dewhurst

'I met a girl, her grandparents used to live in the same village as me and she used to write and tell me how great Wigan was and how friendly it was. So I thought, check this out and being a champion gymnast when I was much younger and having seen the guys at the rugby club dancing I thought, Yeah I can do this no problem. I walked into Wigan for the very first time, I looked at the dance floor and I thought I don't think I'll bother, these guys are something else. They were unbelievable. The atmosphere and the energy put into it was unbelievable.

'It was like somebody had punched you in the face when you opened that door to go into the main hall.'

Gilly

'It was the smell of Brut and sweat all mixed in. That was Wigan's smell.'

Tats – original soul fan

'That's correct and the Torch smell was Armani for the chaps and Estée Lauder for the girls.'

Brian Taylor

'Now at Blackpool Mecca you had the better sounds. Ian Levene and Colin Curtis were great. Levene would play the music he had got from America and Colin was the king of the one-off records. He had about fifty in his bag and they were way ahead. No doubt about it. At the Mecca people were far more serious about the music. They knew that the only way to hear these records was to go to Blackpool and they did.'

Ian Dewhurst

'But before Levene there was Les Cockell and that's who we used to go and hear because he was an ex-Twisted Wheel DJ. He was a brilliant guy, Les. He brought loads of records. We'd get on the bus and go to Blackpool with all the old pensioners on this weekend thing and start taking our dex and our bombers, start chatting to these old people as we got into Blackpool . . . '

Dave Clegg

'There were some damned good songs played at Wigan and some damned crap as well. I loved it all the time. I think one or two of the members in the background were trying to make it commercial, make some money out of it and we didn't want any of that. This was something we did and we wanted it to be ours and stay that way.'

Gilly

THE SOUL STYLISTS

'At Blackpool people started leaving early so they could get to Wigan. I started deejaying there after about six months and it was dynamite. You've got something like 1,500 kids dancing like dervishes and the atmosphere was electric. Because of this Russ decided that Wigan should just be stompers or very fast records. When Levene started bringing in funkier stuff at Blackpool, like "Music Maker" by King Sporty, Russ banned that record from Wigan. You couldn't play it there. It had to be stompers and to be fair you could see his point. Levene actually played Wigan a couple of times and both times he did not carry the crowd. His was a completely different thing.'

Ian Dewhurst

'I felt that at Blackpool Mecca there was definitely a clique. I always felt that I was underdressed when I went there, that I didn't have the money to mix with those people. I thought it was a middle-class thing, Blackpool Mecca. At Wigan I fitted in. It was really dark, no one looked at you, no one gave a shit if you had tuppence in your pocket or two hundred quid. You weren't judged by your bank balance but by your character.'

Dave Prest

'There was a hierarchy. It was elitism. A lot of it was what you've done and where you've been and how long you have been doing it. There are people who haven't been to an all-nighter for twenty years but if they went tomorrow they'd be in there and vice versa.'

Brian Taylor

'I always wanted to be an old boy. I can remember being in Wigan Record Bar looking through the records and not really knowing what they were and thinking, "God I can't wait to get the knowledge".'

Tats

'Eighteen months after its start, Winstanley and the club manager started an off shoot club called Mr M's which took place in the annexe off the main hall. More DJs were now drafted in. Dave Evison got the residency at Mr M's which was about a third of the size of the main club. But they also got in other DJs as well to help him out and personally I think they lost it a bit then.'

Ian Dewhurst

'These guys used to frequent the gap between the balcony and Mr M's. You could tell they were like old muscle boys and if you got something they wanted you wouldn't have any choice, they would take it off you. They were pretty good because they always gave you the first opportunity of buying it back as well. I personally never had any trouble but maybe that's because I was too small for them to want any item of my clothing.'

Gilly

'When people say they were living for the weekend they were not joking. They literally were. You'd finish work at five on a Friday night, get home, get yourself bathed and washed then pack a bag if you were out for a proper weekend.

That's where the carrying of bags comes from because once you got out on a Friday night there was every possibility that you wouldn't get back home until Sunday night. You always had a sense of unity because along the way to various clubs all over England you were constantly meeting like-minded people.'

Ian Dewhurst

* * *

Fashion-wise, the northern scene had moved as far away as possible from its original Modernist roots although some still sported the Mohair and the Ben Sherman style. But for many, particularly the younger generation, change was afoot. Hair was long, much longer, and the choice of clothes was dictated by their extravagant dancing. Therefore, smart shirts had been replaced by vests or loose t-shirts and Levi Sta-prest made way for a much baggier style.

* * *

'The biggest change on the scene from a fashion point of view was the wearing of Skinner jeans. Prior to them, trousers had been Sta-prest followed by Toniks but Skinners were different. Offhand I can't think of any other article that was made a fashion item on the scene as opposed to being adopted by it. I mean, Ben Shermans, Fred Perry, blazers, Crombie coats, Royal brogues, loafers, bomber jackets, long leather coats and so on were fashion items we took as our own. But Skinners – nobody else wore Skinners. Nobody else would dare. I remember getting my first pair which meant travelling from Corby to a shop called Stonedry in Birmingham. You'd get to this shop and there would be soulies from Nottingham, Leicester and all over the Midlands as this was the only outlet for them.'

Brian Taylor

* * *

Also popular was a trouser brand called Spencers. Spencers came in a variety of styles. These included high waisters with 23 buttons, or Oxford-style bags in denim, cotton, and the most prized of all, in blue corduroy. They were mainly sold in Piece Hall Market, Halifax. Also in favour were leather-soled shoes and holdall bags festooned with patches advertising various clubs and containing towels, fresh clothes and talcum powder to sprinkle on the floor to make dancing easier. The world at large was finally given a glimpse of this look and lifestyle in 1974. This was the year that the rock press ran explanatory articles on a scene which had mushroomed under their very noses. By the following year, the estimated attendance of Northern Soul clubs was reaching the 100,000 mark.

This was due in no small part to the commercial efforts of Russ

Winstanley at the Wigan Casino. He had been instrumental in issuing a single entitled 'Footsee' by Wigan's Chosen Few. It became a Top Ten hit in January 1975. To promote it, Northern Soul dancers were invited into *Top Of The Pops* to dance to the tune. Not long after the television cameras – against the stated wishes of its clientele – came to visit the Casino for a documentary on Wigan town, the Casino and soul.

* * *

'We didn't want them coming up. It used to annoy us a lot because certain records were getting onto *Top Of The Pops* and I blame that on Winstanley and the other guy, Jerry Marshall. He had the custody of the building and they wanted to make some money out of it – which I suppose you can't blame them for – but we didn't want to see this kind of thing on TV. It was our scene, it was meant to be underground and that's where it should have stayed. At first, the TV show brought a hell of a lot of people in but when that settled down and, basically, after about two years the numbers started dwindling.'

Gilly

* * *

Indeed, the hardcore and the purists now walked away from the scene, disgusted at its commercialism and the attendant crassness that such attitudes always bring.

* * *

'At the end of the day the people in the record bar at Wigan were the nucleus of the Northern scene.'

Tats

'Playing the *Hawaii Five-0* theme, the *Joe 90* theme and all that shit. It was outrageous. All the dancers were loving it, lapping it up but to the serious guys who frequented the record bars it was a joke, an absolute joke.'

Gilly

'The divvies took it over. They started playing silly music, 'Hawaii Five-0' and all that. That's when we went to other places because once it becomes legal it loses its edge. Once it becomes the norm it loses it.'

Brian Taylor

'It was disgusting. They were trying to get in the last rake of money. I mean the place itself was diabolical – the wiring system, the health and safety of it all – the place had done its time but they took the piss out of the punters towards the end. They had three closing nights. There was actually an all-nighter on in Wigan on the last one and I went to that alternative one. It was an unfair way to go out, if you like.'

Gilly

* * *

By 1977, the Northern Soul scene had lost many of its members. Granted, many of them were never going to last the course anyway whether the scene followed a commercial route or not. But the overt selling of the scene had turned off a large amount of die-hard soul fans and it was their absence that was most keenly felt.

The scene did not die, it just settled into a groove and the years passed. In 1979, a new interest in '60s Modernism was picked up on by the media. This generation now started investigating the Northern scene, giving it an impetus that was previously lacking.

* * *

THE SOUL STYLISTS

'It brought along a right load of idiots. I remember Pat Brady deejaying and saying, "This goes out to all the present-day Mods," and he played Kenny Gamble's "The Joke's On You". But it did leave behind some decent people, people who said, Sod all this revival lark let's take this seriously. And that was good for the scene. Then there was people like Guy Heneghan and Keb Debarge who started the Stafford thing and that was absolutely brilliant. It was things like that which got the scene moving again.'

Gilly

* * *

In 1979, Ady Croasdell and Randy Cozens started the 6T's club in Covent Garden attracting the familiar faces and a smattering of Mod revivalists. A year later they moved to London's famous 100 Club and established a night which many now believe is the best in the country. On some local radio stations there are shows dedicated to the music. Clubs exist in many parts of the country and sell out easily. Northern Soul is truly time-proof. Because it has always been driven by the music, a series of quite amazing records that in just three minutes can leave you breathless with excitement, it survives. At its best, this is music that triggers an enormous amount of feelings. It can drive you onto the dance floor or it can transport you to places you never knew existed. Which is why it will never wither. Plus its appeal is double-edged, with the scene placing its emphasis on either utter enjoyment – dancing, dressing up, adventures into the night – or the eternal hunt for the perfect seven-inch single. Time has not stood still within the scene but it hasn't interfered either. And in many ways Northern Soul has proved to be the friendly face of Modernism. Perhaps because its roots lie in the north, there is far more focus put on friendship with little time for pretension.

* * *

'What's it brought me? Pleasure. Absolute pleasure. I've been so lucky, going to Detroit and meeting a lot of people who are my heroes. Met loads of other people as well, brilliant people and that's why I never wanted it to be a business. If I had a record that somebody else liked more than I did, I would give it to them, I'd never sell it. I've never wanted to make any money out of it. I think it's been a scene – not totally but in parts – where some kids have replaced emotions that may have been lost in life with music. I'm one of them and I know others who are too, where we have replaced loss of emotion with this amazing music. It fills the gap in a lot of lives.'

Gilly

'One of my favourite quotes about Northern Soul is from this guy called Pete Lawson. One night he said to me, "I had forty quid on me this afternoon so I've bought some records and bought some gear. The only thing is I've gone and blown the rest."'

Tats

THE SOUL STYLISTS

CHAPTER FIVE

KEEP IT IN THE FAMILY

SOUL MUSIC TRIUMPHED HEAVILY IN BRITAIN. The British adored the sound of black America. How could they not? It was a music that was simultaneously dynamic and heartbreaking. It could be as rough as wire wool and as elegant as creased mohair trousers. In the late '60s and early '70s it also proved to be groundbreaking. Say it loud for the proud, this period in black American music produced some of its most fertile music.

It began in 1967 when James Brown invented funk music with a string of records that heralded the start of an invincible period in his career. He could do no wrong. Brown worked like no other. Gig after gig all over America, often entering studios at four in the morning to lay down a new idea. Fines for any musician playing a wrong note. Wowing audiences with his amazing dances. He was the self-proclaimed Godfather and no way was he going to allow anyone a shot at his title. Funk was his domain. Because he had invented the stuff with records such as 'Sex Machine' and what's more he understood it like no other. Funk, he had come to realise watching the ecstatic faces in the front row of his concerts night after night, spelled sex and abandonment. That's why he was forever inserting chants into his records. Lyric wise, you really didn't need much else. And by switching the focus of the rhythm away from the drums and bass and onto the guitars and horns, he discovered a music that was earthy and strong and cutting edge. It was a sound that appealed to everything and your brain. Funk could never be pretty and it could never be nice. It relied on repetition and strong syncopation. By 1972, the best clubs in London were the ones playing the funk.

* * *

'Many of the black clubs tended to be reggae clubs, not R&B or soul. But there were some exceptions. There used to be one in Wardour Street Mews and there was another one called Columbo's which was at 50 Carnaby Street. Tough men got shot in there but the music was always cutting edge. Hamilton Bohannon played there when he came out. Juggy Jones, "Inside America" Al Green, The Chi-Lites, a lot of Philly and Stax stuff. It was just at the dawn of that jazz funk thing – Donald Byrd's "Change (Makes You Wanna Hustle)", Van McCoy's "The Hustle", the Fatback Band and a lot of independent stuff like Dooley Silverspoon's "Funky Baby". The first place in the West End to play this music regularly was the 100 Club. It used to be on a Thursday night and it was called Bluesville's House Of Funk. This was the back-end of 1973 and it featured all the latest American imports. Everything was new. Ronnie Earl, who used to run it with his wife, was an old man, must have been in his fifties then. He used to deejay and he was so on top. When he retired he brought in this black guy and his name was Greg Edwards but to be honest Ronnie's music was much better, much more black and funky. The club was 90 per cent black and for me that was unheard of. The crowd was this great mix of gays, gangsters, prostitutes and gamblers.'

Norman Jay – DJ

* * *

In the early '70s, reggae was a major facet in London's hidden soundtrack. It was sold in specialist shops, rarely performed live and mainly heard at midnight council estate parties known as blues dances where all the furniture would be removed and food and drink supplied. Given the resistance to their presence at mainstream clubs the black community had no choice but to provide for themselves.

* * *

'There was nowhere to go but to blues dances. Back then clubs and discos had a fairly racist door policy. You knew that at certain places if you turned up at a certain time they would say, "We've got our quota in." I remember going to Scamps in Hemel Hempstead one night. We knew the guys on the door and they let us in but they were shaking their heads. About twenty minutes later we came out and they said, "We knew you wouldn't last long in there". So we arranged our own things. Every sound system had its own place where it had its blues dances. Everything was two bob. It was two bob to get in, it was two bob for a drink and it was two bob for a plate of curry. Sometimes you saw some mad white guy in there but you rarely saw white women.'

Lloyd Bradley

'There was a chain of pubs called The Bird's Nest. There were ones in West Hampstead, Chelsea and West Kensington. Now there was no way they would have a black night in the King's Road but the West Kensington and West Hampstead ones did and so we gravitated towards them.'

Norman Jay

'We were younger. We were going to school with a load of white kids so we crossed over. What happened was that after we started being able to get into mainstream clubs, black clubs went mainstream, places like The Cobweb or Spinners or Bluesville in Wood Green. The styles then started changing because we were mixing.'

Lloyd Bradley

Another major shift in British black culture took place in 1972 with the release of Gordon Park's film, *Shaft*. For the first time cinema made a young hip black the hero and precipitated the explosion in cinema known as Blaxploitation films. *Shaft* for many young blacks all over the world was a liberating tale about a black detective, so hip in words and style, who was as mean as anyone and – crucially – fought back against all his enemies. Shaft was bad. He didn't dress conventionally, leather jackets and sporting an Afro – but his influence was huge.

* * *

'I was sixteen when *Shaft* came out and that was one of the most exciting things in my life up until then. What happened was that *Shaft* and all those other films gave us a manifestation of blackness that didn't come from Jamaica. There is no indigenous black culture here. We can only take influences from outside, and at the point when James Brown and those films happened, suddenly we had a whole new look. Overnight, we went from Tonik suits and razor cut hair to Afros, flares and tank tops. The Soulboy was born about this time.'

Lloyd Bradley

* * *

The *Shaft* look swept black New York and London too. It caught on through other channels as well, not least the huge success of the Jackson Five whose wardrobe was filled with flares, waistcoats, brightly coloured shirts, beads, all topped off by huge Afro haircuts. This mirrored the shift in influence from the upper echelons of fashion to the pop world where the performer's clothes now took on an extra importance. The early '70s saw a move away from tight, masculine clothing to a looser look. The popularity of long hair, flared trousers and brightly coloured items such as tank tops is just one example of this process. Meanwhile, a new breed of

THE SOUL STYLISTS

funk-driven bands – Kool and The Gang, Ohio Players, Commodores – appeared in the record racks of major import shops. Other developments were also taking place within the genre of soul music. The early work of Barry White, with his use of strings and grand arrangements, had laid the ground for the disco movement which would soon gather force through musicians such as Biddu and Van McCoy. By the mid '70s, disco had become the dominant sound within black American music. In Philadelphia, the setting up of the Sound of Philadelphia records by Kenny Gamble and Leon Huff would bring the two songwriter/producers incredible success. They married catchy vocal melodies to a musical backdrop of driving strings and prominent rhythms and beats. Many of their tunes dealt with the heartache and joy of love. But some highlighted other issues. 'Wake Up Everybody' by Harold Melvin and the Bluenotes, or 'For The Love Of Money' by the O-Jays being prime examples of soul's protest tradition being beautifully upheld. Major musicians such as Marvin Gaye and Stevie Wonder had also striven to get away from the classic '60s soul sound with their – particularly in Stevie's case – use of synthesisers, and, ditto Marvin, heavy orchestration. Their clothes at the time – Stevie's African robes and Marvin's hippy chic look – exemplified this approach. Soul had started to open up and London was quick to embrace these changes.

* * *

'We went to the Bird's Nest in West Hampstead, the Q Club, Paddington, Colombo's (which used to be the Roaring '20s) and the Whiskey A Go Go. That was so rough. Scary rough. The place was full of pimps and dealers. I went there a couple of times and I didn't like it. Upstairs at Ronnie's was the place. Upstairs at Ronnie's was brilliant. It really was the King Of Clubs.'

Lloyd Bradley

* * *

THE SOUL STYLISTS

Of course, dancing was just one part of it. Acquiring these records was equally as important. Which is where the Contempo record shop played its part. In the Mod tradition it was hidden from view, situated in a small street behind Oxford Street. No big neon signs waving at your wallet. You had to work to find this shop.

* * *

'Going to Contempo's was like a religious experience. It was above a bar called Bradley's Bar in Hanway Street. Blues and soul was at the back and Contempo was in the front. It was all owned by John Abbey and it was about the only place you could get singles at about the time they were released in America. That was Contempo. The records normally came in on a Friday and by the time they had cleared customs and arrived at the shop it would be about 1 p.m. so that was the time you got there. The bloke behind the counter would play the tunes and you'd stand there with loads of other people listening. If you liked the tune you would nod and he'd put it in a pile for you. Once in a while, you'd say, "How much have I got there?" so you'd know how much you had left to spend – or not as the case may be.

Not a lot of talking went on. Occasionally, you would ask for something but the chances were you probably couldn't get to the counter to ask. Friday was not the best day for asking. Friday, you heard the new tunes. The reggae shops had a similar system, but on a Saturday morning. Friday you got your funk and soul, Saturday you got your reggae and the exact same performance would go on in the reggae shop as it did in Contempo.'

Lloyd Bradley

'I remember hearing this tune that Ronnie played at the 100 Club and then on Friday going into Contempo and loads of people in there all singing the chorus of "Shame Shame Shame".'

Norman Jay

In 1975, builders finally finished renovation work at 80 Dean Street and within the week a club called Crackers was opened to the public. It would be gone by the '80s but all who went retain their memories in that special part of the mind. Crackers was important to many people, its name resonates to this day.

* * *

'Mark Roman was the first DJ there. George Power was later. It had a slightly different edge to the 100 Club. The 100 Club was more chart led.'

Norman Jay

'The Friday lunchtime session was great. Everybody had jobs in offices or whatever and you would see them with ties in their pockets giving it plenty. It was weird. You would come out of there at 2.30 and it would be bright sunshine. You couldn't see for five minutes. I was a chef at the time so I'd be down there in my chef clothes. Nobody gave a fuck. And if you could wangle the time off work you would go there for the lunchtime session and then you'd go up to Contempo and get some tunes. On Friday afternoon hardly anyone went to work.'

Lloyd Bradley

'At clubs like Crackers a lot of the black kids also went to football as well. People like Babsie, top guy at Chelsea, the Burns Brothers from Arsenal, Nat and Tiny from Millwall, all of them soulboys.'

Terry Farley – DJ

'If you were into buying tunes Mark Ryman the DJ was playing everything you should have bought the week before. He was always ahead and you were always struggling to keep up. He conditioned the crowd there to be always on the edge musically. Crackers quickly got the reputation for the best dancers and the most fashionable black kids because this was the only place we could go and dance and wear the gear.'

Norman Jay

'You had the dance floor and you had to be a great dancer to get on. Outside the dance floor were people who could dance but weren't quite good enough and then you had the people who couldn't dance at all and they stood right at the back. It did open on a Saturday night but we were about sixteen or seventeen and on Saturday they were looking for drinkers. None of us drank really. Everyone just had enough for a coke and the train fare to get there.'

Paul McKee – video commissioner

'I went to the dance centre and Pineapple studios to learn jazz ballet simply because my friends used to take the piss out of me propping the bar up. I could move but I had to learn because you were recognised for doing moves.'

Ean Carter – soulboy

'When I first went to Crackers I was about sixteen and a half. Everyone was wearing vintage clothes in there. There was a stall near the King's Road and they did loads and loads of second-hand pegs. They were usually dark blue, mainly dark colours and people used to wear plastic sandals with them and second-hand bowling shirts with people's names on their back. What happened then was that Acme Attractions and McLaren's Sex Shop started making clothes for that scene and people started getting a little more outrageous. I bought a pair of pink pegs and my mate Gary Haisman had a pair of red ones with sparkles in them. And those two shops for about a year were soulboy shops.'

Terry Farley

'I had been earning a fair old living just deejaying, doing clubs and parties.

One Sunday night I was working in the Horse and Cock when a guy came up to me and said he was the manager of a place called The Goldmine in Canvey Island. In those days it was one of those discotheques that had a band that played two sets and the DJ did three sets. He asked me if I'd be interested in playing at his place. I told him I would if they changed their musical policy.

'I can't remember the band's name but I had them doing Motown covers and they did a blinding version of "I'm Doing Fine Now". But eventually they became redundant because the music was far more important than the band playing. The manager said it would be more cost effective if he just had a DJ. I insisted that we called this thing a soul night or a soul club in response to the fact that we didn't want people from the island coming. We realised that most of the people on the island resented people coming into it so to avoid any trouble we just wouldn't let them in. I had the best Monday in the world.

'No one has ever had a Monday like it since. There used to be coaches outside on a Monday night. People couldn't believe you could get that many people to come on a Monday. That's when the manager said to me, "I want you to do Thursday, Friday, Saturday and Sunday."'

Chris Hill

* * *

Soul had got darker with funk and it now began to experiment with serious musicians who attempted to fuse jazz into its main body. Jazz-funk, as it was called, was the result of records made by the likes of Donald Byrd, Kool and the Gang, Maze, Grover Washington Jnr, Lonnie Liston Smith and others. They usually featured a catchy rhythm and long musical workouts punctuated by jazz styled solos. If the darker edge of funk was the Crackers sound, then jazz funk was the sound of the Goldmine.

* * *

THE SOUL STYLISTS

'Because we were all into self-expression, we were into jazz-funk. Jazz is self-expression – it's open your mind and think for yourself. Every time I hear the same tune I get a different interpretation of that tune whether it be Ronnie Law's "Always There" or Willie Bobo's "Always There". You get different feelings every time you hear those records.'

Ean Carter

'When we got to the Goldmine I was shocked. I was expecting it to be a black club. I was the only black guy in there so I got a bit paranoid. I thought the music was fantastic but I hated the vibe. I felt tension all night. We left before the end. And then we realised that Sunday night was our night and that was more like it. The music was wicked but a little safe. I liked the ghetto-edged music. They played similar music at the 100 Club but with a definite difference in attitude plus the Goldmine didn't have the dancers there. I was used to people being on the tip. At the 100 Club, as soon as "The Bus Stop" came on, everyone could do it. As soon as "The Hustle" came on, everybody could do it. That was the essential difference. They would like "Expansions" by Lonnie Liston Smith whilst we would be into "Johannesburg" by Gil Scott Heron.'

Norman Jay

'The crowd divided themselves into tribes. There was the Dimlows, the Catholic River Wideners, the Funky Chicks, the Brixton frontline Magnum Force. They used to get T-shirts done up with their names on them or make their own bags. Some of them were quite tough. I tell you, you didn't want to fuck around with the Magnum Force.'

Chris Hill

'The only violence we had was over the prejudice thing. People who were with what they thought was their young lady would get a little annoyed when a mate of ours or someone dancing in the circle dropped some good moves and the young lady went and danced with him. The next thing you find out is that the guy doesn't like girls dancing with members of the ethnic minority. I had my teeth smashed in one night simply because I had a West Indian friend.'

Ean Carter

'I had problems on Canvey Island. I used to get called all kinds of things. There were all these white girls who lived in the area having it off with a load of black guys. I remember this horrible DJ went onto some local radio station having a go at me. He was saying things like, "You're the one bringing all the coons into the area." I had hate mail, National Front stuff. Must have been doing something right.'

Chris Hill

* * *

Chris Hill's following was immense and grew without any mainstream press save that of publications such as *Blues and Soul*. His crowd was mixed, mainly white but always out for a good time. They dressed outlandishly, unrecognisable from the Ivy League look their elders once sported. Instead, they opted for a look that consisted of plastic sandals, trousers that were leather or certainly much roomier than before and mohair jumpers. Other items would have included Fiorucci capped T-shirts, boxing boots, denim dungarees, tank tops, loud Hawaiian or bowling shirts, high-waisted trousers and spats shoes. The last had come into fashion following the 1974 release of the film *The Great Gatsby*. Some Goldmine regulars sought to replicate a part of the 1920s look. Again, it was a long way from the straight masculine look that had dominated the '60s although its unisex nature offended some.

* * *

'Make no mistake. If you wore that stuff, within the black community at least, you were gay. Some of my mates would put their clothes in a bag because they couldn't leave the house dressed like it. My mates would change downstairs at Tottenham Court Road. They'd be pulling out their mohair jumpers as people were coming off the platforms.'

Norman Jay

* * *

Soulboy hair was often cut in a wedge style, an invention of hairdresser Ricci Burns, in which the hair is graduated and swept across the forehead. It was a cut appropriated by David Bowie for his *Young Americans* (1975) album cover; a work, in fact, that saw Bowie, then a huge international star, attempting to place himself firmly within a soulboy context. Bowie was not the first to be attracted to this vibrant but secretive scene.

* * *

'Anthony Price and Bryan Ferry came down The Goldmine one night. They wanted to shoot a video in there with the punters. I refused because of the music. It wasn't the right music. If you bought me Billy Paul, fine. Not fine, great. If you bought me Bobby Womack, great. But not Bryan Ferry.'

Chris Hill

* * *

In 1975 Chris Hill introduced a half hour of big band music into his set. He did so to add a new element of fun to the proceedings. Maybe he wouldn't have bothered had he known that it would start the process which would kill the Goldmine.

* * *

'The dramatic change was in 1975 when they all went into glamour. I started doing this half-hour set which they called the Glenn Miller

(American big band leader) half hour even though it wasn't. I was playing stuff like Louis Prima and black big band R&B which was jiving music.'

Chris Hill

* * *

Word of young people dancing to old music is always enough to interest the media. Certainly, it was enough to bring *Vogue* and *Melody Maker* to the Goldmine doors, eager to write about young kids wearing retro clothes and dancing to old time music. The writers concerned discovered girls wearing Swanky Mode clothes and oozing 1920s sleaziness and guys sporting military wear, shirts with stripes and epaulettes, looking like American GIs. (Bryan Ferry also styled this look on various TV and concert appearances.) The resulting publicity helped sell the Goldmine to a wider world but by concentrating on the retro element, its function as a major British soul club was ignored.

* * *

'The swing thing got so big I thought, I'm in a trap here. I'm getting known as a DJ who plays swing music. Well, I only played it for a little bit, the rest of the time I'm playing soul and jazz. I was the first one to play jazz to a large room and that was fusion stuff like Grover Washington but also, "Milestones" by Miles Davis or "Theme From *Alfie*" by Sonny Rollins. I was also the first one to start playing Brazilian music. I used to play bongos and bells on stage. I had a floor that thought everything I did was wonderful so the trick was to stay ahead. Anyway, the guy who managed the Goldmine left to manage this place called the Lacy Lady in Ilford. He rang me up and said, "Look you've done everything you can do at The Goldmine. Why don't you start again?"'

Chris Hill

* * *

THE SOUL STYLISTS

The offer came in 1976, the year that would see this soul scene touch upon a new rock movement, Punk rock, now starting to gain momentum in the music press. Certainly, many future musicians – John Lydon, Sade, Alison Moyet, Siouxsie Sioux – would later reveal themselves as Goldmine regulars. Other not so famous regulars would be present at early Punk shows and thus the mohair jumper, leather trousers and plastic sandals look would form the basis of the Punk's wardrobe. It was the Lacy Lady, the club that Chris moved to, that would encourage this crossover.

* * *

'That audience was the weirdest looking audience. We were the only club to open on Christmas Day and I made a rule that everyone had to come dressed in their wrapping paper for Xmas. So everyone turned up wearing polythene bags, bin liners and all held together by safety pins. I don't know whether that was a happy coincidence or not, but that then became the uniform of Punk. The Clash played the Lacy once. Bernie Rhodes their manager came to me and he said, "You've got to put The Clash on. This is the one gig they've got that to do." I said musically, it wouldn't work. He went, it will and he was right because the Punk kids were the soul kids at the cutting edge.'

Chris Hill

'We used to go to a club in Maidenhead called Skindles and there was a guy called Alan Sullivan who was a soul boy. He used to be one of the leaders of the shed. He was called Sully. He left all that behind and he got into soul and he also started playing a lot of funk. There was a gang of kids from Reading and they were all dressed in these sexy clothes and I remember one week this kid came in with his record and he said to Sully, "You've got to play this record." He put it on and it was "Anarchy In The UK" by the Sex Pistols. There were four kids pogoing and about 50 other kids standing there watching. After about thirty seconds, Alan took it off, smashed it in two and said, "This is not soul!"'

Terry Farley

'I was never comfortable with marrying the two but from a fashion point-of-view that's where it was happening. Plastic sandals, mohair jumpers and trousers that were pegged. I've got to say it was the most sexually charged atmosphere.'

Chris Hill

'Louise's – where they say all the Punks hung out – Gary Haisman took me down there and that was a lesbian club where all the soul boys went. Even though everyone was 16 or 17 it was cool to be gay. A lot of the black guys who were the best dancers acted gay. It turned out none of them were but they certainly acted it. A lot of people did.'

Terry Farley

* * *

Punk didn't swallow up too many soul boys and girls. In 1977, Janet Street Porter, herself an ex-Mod, took the LWT cameras into a busy Goldmine for a short documentary. Later on, Danny Baker in the *NME* wrote about the scene, telling his readers that Chris Hill was a man of the people who didn't need the press to succeed. Another 'man of the people' was Capital Radio's Greg Edwards who hosted a Saturday night show called *Soul Spectrum*.

It was two hours of pure Goldmine music, the one show everyone involved stayed in to catch before heading out for the dance floors. Magazine wise you turned to *Blues and Soul* or the late James Hamilton's column in *Record Mirror*. There was nothing else save the odd piece in the rock press once every five years.

'By then we had formed our own underground all around the West End. You didn't read about these clubs, you just knew about them.'

Norman Jay

'It was because the glamour thing had gone, the soul mob didn't have an identity anymore. So they started to dress up in silly clothes rather than follow some fashion thing.'

Chris Hill

* * *

Fancy dress, rather than the kind of cutting-edge fashion which the scene had promoted now took prominence. The fashion sense was put aside to make way for boys and girls in togas.

* * *

'I think it was that people had gotten a bit sick of the fashion thing and by dressing up in fancy dress clothes that levelled everyone out. You couldn't be judged in fancy dress whereas you could with normal clothing.'

Steven Harris – author

* * *

The scene splintered in the late '70s. Some opted for the West End funk scene that was being pioneered at clubs like Le Beat Route and which bled into the New Romantic era. Some stayed on and some were left to immerse themselves in the Casual movement. Like all soul scenes, there were remnants left behind. But its power, its impetus was gone.

* * *

THE SOUL STYLISTS

'You never look backwards. At that age, why would you? This is what's happening now. You need the music to go with the clothes, to go with the lifestyle, to go with the attitude. Forwards. No looking back.'

Norman Jay

THE SOUL STYLISTS

CHAPTER SIX

The unbroken circle

'At first sight these youths look like an undifferentiated mass, but nothing could be further from the truth. If you knew what to look for, you could see that they were engaged in a kind of style war, the like of which has not been seen since the original Mod era of the '60s.'

New Society, 30 June 1983

* * *

WATCHING. MICK MAHONEY IS WATCHING. He stands on Euston train station, body tensed up as he diligently surveys the scene. Placed around him are about a hundred Chelsea fans. Under normal conditions they would be the enemy. Not today. Today, they have joined forces with Mick and about forty other Arsenal boys and they are watching. Watching the arrival of the Manchester train carrying United fans. Pretty soon, they will assault the Mancunians, give them a kicking that the fuckers will never ever forget.

The air is taut. Nerves are jangling. One hundred and forty young football fans, all schooled in violence. Some with scars, some without. They are dispersed into pockets of ten or fewer, are scattered around the platform. They wait and watch as the United supporters disembark and start walking noisily towards them. Some Northern songs fill the air and the London boys quickly turn their heads away from the oncoming army and pretend to act casual, hide the fear and the excitement bubbling up inside them now.

Mick looks around and suddenly it hits him: nothing is going to go off. He can just sense it. There's far more United fans than they had counted on and looking at his troops he sees that there's no one with The Look in their eye, The Look that precedes serious violence, the one that says, 'FUCK IT. I DON'T CARE. I'M GOING IN.' Mick hasn't got that look. No one else has either.

Mick even has time to think to himself, 'Fuck sake, the amount of times we take the piss out of the Northerners for the way they dress and here they are walking straight past us and not even suspecting we're the enemy. And for what? Because we dress exactly the same as them.'

The thought hits him hard. 'For fuck sake. We are as badly dressed as the Northerners!'

Mick has long hair styled à la Rod Stewart. He wears baggy jeans, a blue jumper with a tartan scarf and he wears brothel creepers. His jeans cover his shoes. That's important. Truth be told, he doesn't want to move until all the United fans have swept past him. If the United boys see his shoes – bought that week from Ravel – that will give away his London identity and trigger their rage. By the time his mates get to him, many of whom are now slipping quietly away, it will be too late.

So Mick Mahoney stands still and covers his shoes and helplessly watches as the United fans fill up the station and the likelihood of one person – just one person – making the first move diminishes accordingly. And then the vision arrives. From out of nowhere. And it's amazing. Pure. And strong. And at what a moment!

Flung eagerly into the train-scented air are a host of strong, loud voices and they sing, 'We are the famous, the famous Millwall, we are the famous, the famous Millwall.'

Excitedly, Mick turns expecting to see a hundred dockers, the usual Millwall supporter. But he's fooled. Instead he sees a man whose appearance will be embedded in his mind until the day he dies. This man wears a panama hat over his ginger hair, a bright green luminous bowling shirt, baggy trousers with a thin belt at the top of them, black and white spats and his teeth, it seems, are all made of gold. Behind him, his mates follow and they all wear different coloured berets. It's fucking outrageous. Mick's never seen anything like it in his life. These Millwall guys are not only going to take on the United bunch but their dress sense actually matches their outlandish behaviour. 'We are the famous, the famous Millwall.'

Mick is seventeen and already he has seen a lot. But this spectacle has him rooted to the spot.

The next week he decides to investigate Millwall. He lives in Tufnell Park and he supports Arsenal. But now, whenever he can, he will go to the Millwall because the guys he saw on Euston platform – well, that's what he wants to look and act like. For the rest of his life. It's just that he didn't know it until now.

And at Millwall, that's where he discovers the Casuals.

* * *

'I think the Casual thing was more underground or revolutionary than Punk. Punk was orchestrated but this was anti-fashion. I mean, I used to get really drunk on a Saturday afternoon and then go to the pie and mash shop on Tower Bridge Road and eat loads of pie and mash with the aim of getting fatter. That was because the clothes didn't look any good if you were skinny.'

Mick Mahoney – playwright

* * *

On one fact we can all be agreed. The Casual look – a mix of sportswear and designer clothes – was nourished and given its direction on the football terraces by the usual hierarchy of top Faces and their followers. Try and discover its actual birthplace and that's when the arguments start.

Whilst Mick Mahoney and a million other Londoners have no hesitation in guiding you to South East London to show you its birthplace, the author

Kevin Sampson takes you elsewhere. He states that at the Charity Shield game between Liverpool and Southampton, which took place at the start of the 1976–77 season, he was intrigued to see a few Liverpool fans wearing a whole new style of dress. Gone were the usual Flemings trousers, unattractive parallel trousers worn with boots, that had been much in evidence at Liverpool's last game away at Wolverhampton. These style setters completed The Look with Adidas T-shirts and trainers. Their haircuts were also significant, with side partings that went right across the ear. They didn't look like anything Sampson had ever seen before.

* * *

'There was the big southern-based soulboy look which was the wedge haircut, the mohair jumper and the plastic sandals and those certainly were the elements that were swiped and appropriated and mixed and matched. There were two things that used to mark the mid-'70s. They were centre partings in your hair and wide kegs and that is what most kids were wearing all over the country. Now the only reason I can think of for the fashion leaping in a matter of months is that Liverpool played the UEFA Cup final.

During that campaign we had been to so many places that had good sportswear – Germany in particular, the home of Adidas – and the final itself was in Bruges and those places were quite easy to rob from. The other thing to remember is that there's always been strange little scenes going on in Liverpool and I think it's partly to do with the amount of culture that came in through the docks. There were the Cunard Yanks who were Liverpool lads who went off as merchant seamen and came back with loads of different influences from all over the world. I think that's an interesting parallel with the Casuals later on. Also, in Liverpool in general, there has always been a Mod culture there – urban, working class, stylish, always a uniform and that was the first time I'd seen that particular one. And what came out of it was what was eventually labelled "Casuals".'

Kevin Sampson – author

THE SOUL STYLISTS

'They were such chancers. It was London, 100 per cent London. The original guys were older and they were gangster types, criminals, Cockney cab drivers and the like. That's where it came from. I used to work up Oxford Street with the street traders and they used to all dress like spivs. They were quite old and they were wearing Gabicci tops, Farah trousers and crocodile skin shoes. London, 100 per cent.'

Mick Mahoney

* * *

'The London fans did have that taxi driver look, all bright colours and tomfoolery (jewellery) and nothing wrong with that. But Liverpool wasn't about that. It was about sportswear, about wanting to look like your Dad, like a golfer or Bruce Forsyth or something. That came about because Liverpool Football Club was the only team in Europe at the time so we were travelling round, visiting loads of different cities and shops and then bringing the gear back home well before the London boys.'

Kevin Sampson

* * *

Despite the arguments as to its birthplace it should also be acknowledged that within London's black community a similar style – and at an earlier time – was being developed through the Sticksman style. The Sticksman was the Rude Boy's replacement, although in terms of attitude there was no difference between the two. Sticksmen were young black males who tended to be very aware that British society in the '70s was unlikely to be offering them a lot in the way of education and employment. Urban and working class, living in council estate areas, this generation, like its white counterpart, knew that to gain the clothes and accessories that would give them standing amongst their peers, they would have to live on society's margins. (A good example of this attitude and style is that of the reggae singer, Gregory Isaacs.) Sticksman favoured Italian knitwear, Farah trousers and snakeskin or crocodile skin shoes. It is highly likely that this look originated in Jamaica through the acquisition of second-hand American clothing and was inspired by the respect roughneck Jamaicans have consistently afforded New York Mafia guys. (Martin Scorsese's *Goodfellas*, partly set in the early '70s, has numerous examples of this look as numerous characters parade around in mouth-watering, colourful knitwear.)

* * *

'You mustn't forget travel at this time, particularly in the '70s. This was when people could afford to travel so many of them as in my case went to Jamaica then on to New York which is where they would have seen certain ideas and then brought them back here. For example, at the end of that Spike Lee film, *Crooklyn*, which is set in the '70s, he uses footage from *Soul Train* and a lot of the audience are dressed in sportswear.'

Carol Tulloch

'For some reason, on the Walworth Road there were loads and loads of menswear shops. Don't know why but there were loads of shops selling things like Gabiccis and Farahs. The Casual look was predominantly a reggae one. It started in Jamaica, don't know why but it wouldn't be New York because they were all into that *Shaft* look at the time. This look was based around suede knitwear but it also included giant hats. Bally shoes from Switzerland were massive so were croc skin shoes but also canes, walking canes. The Casual look was a modification of this look.

I mean, check out Gregory Isaacs, I don't think I've ever seen a photo where he is not wearing a Gabicci.'

Norman Jay

'The first time people were aware of Sticksmen was at the Global Village, a club in London round about the mid-'70s.'

Paul McKee

'In London there were the Sticksmen and the guys who were white and dressed like them were called the Chaps. It was an Italian look that the black kids bought and which the white kids nicked. And that was the start of it all.'

Terry Farley

'If you look at the shops where you could buy stuff like Gabicci they were all in heavily populated black areas. Peckham, Stoke Newington, Finsbury Park. You couldn't get them anywhere else.'

Lloyd Bradley

'The thing was you had Peckham and right next to it you've got Bermondsey and they are two very distinctive worlds. Peckham is very black and Bermondsey is very white. But they coexisted and they influenced each other.'

Mick Mahoney

'I remember going over to Millwall with Chelsea and all the Millwall faces were in blazers, Aquascutum shirts, slacks and crocodile shoes.'

Terry Farley

'All I know is that in the late '70s both black and white kids in South London started to wear things like Lois jumbo cords, Farahs, trainers, designer tops. And to be honest a lot of robbing went on to get the stuff. I know all my mates went robbing to get the gear. I myself would go to New York and buy up loads of Lacoste stuff, high quality stuff and bring it back and sell it.

Or my mates would give me a new set of trainers and I would wear them for a week and after a couple of days people would say, "Where did you get those?" And I'd tell them, "Well there's this guy I know . . ."'

Norman Jay

* * *

The inevitable result of the mixing that takes place in schools and later on at work and in clubland meant that it wouldn't be too long before the Sticksman look was adapted by white kids. From there, it was only a small step to the football terraces. In Liverpool The Look differed with a mix of sportswear and name brands such as Lois jeans being favoured and a strong emphasis being placed on the acquisition and displaying of trainers. In Manchester there were further variations, many citing the return of the flared corduroy as a great example of Mancunian style. Furthermore, two other elements now have to be added to the equation. Football and criminality. It is probably fair to say that the Casual movement created more illegal activity than any other youth cult has before or since. The name of the cult — Casual — fully underplayed the attitude that was necessary to acquire the expensive brand names needed to successfully fufil its clothing requirements.

Given its high costs it's not hard to see why.

In the late '70s, Britain suffered from increasingly unstable economic conditions. Unlike their Mod counterparts, the Casuals did not exist within a secure, prosperous society. Going into the '80s jobs were thin on the ground and unemployment amongst the young was high. Margaret Thatcher's divisive economic policies had driven a massive rift between rich and poor.

In the early '80s, therefore, the fashion designer — for example say Katherine Hamnett — was able to assume a position within the media that had not been granted her predecessors, most of whom tended to feature in the pages of *Vogue* and little else. The ethos of money glorification that Thatcher now instilled into British society meant that for those who could afford it designer styles had suddenly become extremely desirable. The wearing of such clothing was a very visible way of displaying to the world your financial status. South Molton Street, near London's Bond Street, duly transformed itself into a Mecca for this moneyed minority. The Casual movement can be seen as a working-class response to this shift in wider society – just as the Mods mimicked their bosses and demanded the best so the Casuals aspired to designer status. Their philosophy stated: *You may come from nothing but you will go to every length to dress like you have everything.*

* * *

'If you could get a Christian Dior suit, a silk shirt from Cecil Gee, a pair of crocodile skin shoes with a gold bar on them, that was great. If you could only get Russell and Bromley shoes, Farah slacks and a Roberto Carlo top that was okay. It was all about looking great, about looking like a million dollars. It was about saying, boom! – I've got the clothes! It doesn't matter how but I'm fucking here!'

Mick Mahoney

* * *

When Mick Mahoney ventured south he discovered a whole new world. He found clubs on the Old Kent Road jammed with great looking women grooving to Donna Summer. He mixed with guys who you never asked what they did for a living. And he found himself intoxicated by the air of criminal wealth that pervaded their hangouts.

* * *

'The Casual thing is the only one that was actually criminal orientated. When you dressed like that it was basically saying, "I am a thief." A lot of us dressed differently in the day because otherwise you were a walking advert. A lot of kids went at it with their Gabicci stuff and their Burberry stuff. But the shrewder ones dressed differently.'

Mick Mahoney

* * *

Like Mods, the Casuals blended so smoothly into society that they went totally unnoticed by the media for years. Their timing was spot on. In 1976, Punk arrived and fully engaged the media's attention, that is the tabloids and the music press. The voracious style press was yet to be invented. No *Face*, no *Arena* in 1976. By the time the media did catch on, the original Casual movement was at its peak and ready to die. Their anonymous style of dress accounts for the lack of photographic evidence of the original participants. Only those who knew the signals, knew the small labels featured on the clothing would have understood its significance and caught this new breed of Mod on camera. Similarly, its subsequent growth on the football terraces remains responsible for its complete absence from the media. The football terrace is where the changes were made, the new fashions first unveiled. Unlike other fashions that are traditionally linked to music this meant that – for the first four years at least – there were no pop groups or successful public figures to represent the Casuals, no mouthy musician to publicise its style and philosophy. It was only at football that the interested observer could get close to them and not many did. Why? Because at this particular juncture, mid-'70s, the beautiful game merited only apathy and distaste from the wider public, thanks to its violent image. The consequence was that Casual culture developed far away from the media spotlight for many, many years.

It may be the last cult that will be allowed to do so.

* * *

'Because what were good about that look were it were that straight that people didn't know what you were doing.'

Dave – original Casual

'It was like a fashion show, an Intercity fashion show . . . it was all about parading and being seen.'

Nigel – original Casual

'The reason why the identity was not revealed until late on was because they were not interested in anybody else apart from supporters of other clubs that they saw at matches.'

Frank Cartledge – lecturer

* * *

In Scotland dress and attire appeared quite late after London. Perhaps the most famous crew were the Aberdeen casuals, althought most major clubs had their quota of Armani-wearing fans. Indeed, the unbridgeable gap between Rangers and Celtic fans was nearly breached through their shared love of clothes and attitude.

* * *

'I knew the head of the Rangers Casuals, a guy called Elvis. It was cool between us but the other Celtic fans did not like us. They chased us down the pitch one day at a game between us and Hibs.'

Richard Simpson – clothes stylist

'It definitely was football but it was happening in the discos as well. Not the trendy clubs in the West End but in localised clubs which attracted the same people that went to football I suppose.'

Mick Robinson – hotel proprietor

THE SOUL STYLISTS

'It was not about famous international designers. The first sportswear I remember everybody wearing on their feet were Dunlop Green Flash and that turned into Adidas which gave people a huge range to pick from. The first ones were the Mamba and the Samba. Forest Hills came shortly after that, then Stan Smiths then the strap-overs which were the first ones to go over £30.'

Kevin Sampson

'Diadora 'Big Elite' which, allegedly, were made out of kangaroo skin, were £35 which in 1980 was a lot of money. After that, people started wearing Burberry macs and then Aquascutum and then they got into Chevignon.'

Terry Farley

'That sportswear thing in London, that was predominantly a black scene and they were doing it before the Scousers and doing it much better. I don't mean to sound down on Scousers because I do like them but they do have delusions. That said, I do remember when I got the wedge haircut which was about 1978 and I was embarrassed about having one 'cos it was kind of late but I couldn't think of another haircut to have. To be fair, Liverpool had them before Arsenal. But the soulboys had them years before.'

Mick Mahoney

'Blacks have always been associated with sportswear. We're good at things like athletics or look at the key basketball players in America who are like Gods. Many of my mates ran for teams such as the Harriers and they would get all the new trainers. So I'd wear them as well. It was just something you did.'

Norman Jay

'Wearing training shoes was quite a radical thing. To start wearing them as a fashion statement it was the kind of thing your mum and dad would have approved of. It's hard to state how revolutionary it was at the time. The only thing I see as remotely similar was The Jam with those bowling shoes.'

Kevin Sampson

'What I would say is that the impetus in the North came from Liverpool or Manchester simply because they were travelling to Europe. From there it dispersed out until at one point every Northern club in whatever division had a small crew of Casuals.'

Frank Cartledge

'Every team by the start of the '80s had their own mob of Casuals. Not necessarily hundreds of them but everyone had a little mob. I remember there was a Futurama gig at Deeside at which there were quite a few fights and I can remember being surprised because I saw quite a few knocking around with Lacoste shirts on. (The first time I had heard of Lacoste was when I read Emanuelle and it was mentioned in the book.) So I assumed they were Scousers but then we heard their accents we realised they were from the North East and I knew then it was spreading.'

Kevin Sampson

'Going abroad at the time was a really trendy thing to do in football. This was the late '70s. Arsenal were often in Europe, so were Spurs. But Chelsea were in the Second Division so that's why Chelsea joined onto England and started following them to away games. Once they got abroad with England they started going to the shops and seeing all the stuff you couldn't get in England. They would steal the clothes or use stolen credit cards to bring them back because there was no checking by computer then.'

Terry Farley

'Because it's football you've got that mobility. Also, if you're watching a third or fourth division side, the football's not going to be that good. So you spend a lot of your time looking at other guys on the terrace.'

Frank Cartledge

'People were really trying to outdo each other. You're wearing Lacoste so we're Armani. You're wearing Armani so we'll get some completely unheard-of designer.'

Kevin Sampson

* * *

Different city, different name. Londoners were Casuals, Liverpool were Scallies and Manchester were the Perry Boys, named after the Fred Perry shirts they wore. But in London – a place where the majority of people arrive rather than a city where people are born and raised – this condition is doubled thanks to football loyalty, the one element that divides a city's inhabitants like no other.

* * *

'I remember once, it was at the start of a season and we were playing Arsenal. We were waiting for them outside a tube station, loads of us young and old. Then they came out and they had on Fila velour tracksuits and we just went, fucking hell. We hadn't seen anything like it. Most of us walked away. The older ones were going, "Come on." But we were going, "Too late, mate, they've already done us on the wardrobe front."'

Terry Farley

'That happened to us at QPR. We'd gone down there to have a go at the Arsenal. I think they were playing some cup match. Anyway, we were waiting for them and then they all came out and they were wearing Armani jumpers going, "You scruffy bastards." And you know what? They were right.'

Norman Jay

'The volume of the violence was massive. I used to leave my house, go to King's Cross and we would have skirmishes with London fans going away.

Then we might get lucky with some Luton or Manchester fans and so a few more skirmishes would develop. Then we'd skirmish with Northerners coming into town, skirmish with them on the tube and outside the ground then we'd wait for the London fans. I mean, you could fight or run all day long. Then at night you could go up the West End and fight there as well!'

Mick Mahoney

'They changed things as quickly as possible so as to keep it alive, keep the impetus. That meant that you had the most amazing stylistic changes occurring, within days even.'

Frank Cartledge

'One week it was like Slazengers were alright and the next week they weren't alright. Then it had to be a checked shirt done up all the way to the top and one week you didn't have to wear any pants. It got as ridiculous as that.'

Tim – Sheffield Casual

'The big boys at the top hardly got into fights. They got the dickheads to run around causing trouble while they were busy making money which never actually got passed down. All the major Casuals that I knew were into timeshare selling or going off and poncing around on beaches, selling gear. I remember this guy I knew, a "Face" if you like and really interesting to talk to, coming back from somewhere or other. I was in this club, saw him, went over and had a chat. Next thing I know people are coming up all night long, saying, "Oh, you know so and so," and I was bought drinks all night long. All because I stood and talked with one of the Faces.'

Frank Cartledge

* * *

It was in Europe, home to many of the much sought after clothing items, that the Casuals often struck gold. In May 1981, Liverpool played Real Madrid in the European Cup Final. Paris steeled itself for the inevitable mayhem and violence. Instead, they found themselves utterly bemused by the Liverpool fans who seemed to have no interest in fighting the opposing team's supporters but preferred to go shopping. They soon learnt. By match-day all of Paris's sports shops had been forced to employ security guards who manned their shop doors and only allowed two people in at a time. The following year, a young Yorkshire guy called Robert Wade Smith opened up his first shop in Liverpool. Wade Smith worked for Peter Black, the main distributor for Marks and Spencer. One of their other clients was Adidas sportswear, an account that Wade Smith started working on in 1977. He was seventeen years old and straight away he noticed that Liverpool was responsible for one third of Adidas's business in Britain.

* * *

'I always wanted to set up my own business, had done since I was fifteen. So I was looking for the right opportunity and this was staring me in the face every week. I worked for Adidas but I was having bad arguments with the Adidas UK people because they thought the bubble was going to burst and that Liverpool was a one-off. They really didn't want to fuel it by bringing in the rare imports. I was arguing that they had to start bringing in the special styles from Austria, Germany, Denmark, Spain, Italy, Holland, France – they all had different styles, especially Germany. There was a lot of different productions going on for different countries and different taste levels. Some of the shoes were pretty ugly – but then Kickers and Pods were pretty ugly – but there was a certain thing about the fact that they were different and you couldn't get them anywhere else. It started with Adidas Stan Smith in 1979. That was a phenomenon. There were something like 10,000 pairs of Stan Smith sold in one shop which is mind-blowing. What followed after that was that it suddenly went up in price. That was the first time that the £19.99 price was created. The average price in the UK was £14.99. It then rose to £29.99 which was just unbelievable but only in Liverpool. That was a range called Wimbledon and Grand Prix and they were tennis shoes with double-density PU soles, a man-made rubberised soul. Ilie Nastase used to wear them. What caused all this was the Liverpool fans travelling around Europe with the football team and they picked up on anything you couldn't get in the UK.

'These were very expensive tennis shoes and it was thought that the UK couldn't stand the price. They were buying them at a lower cost in Germany and that created such a cult back home that there were 5,000 fans who could get them but that left 50,000 Merseyside kids that couldn't get access to them. And that's what created the boom. I had eighteen months of arguing with Adidas. It wasn't that bad but they were fairly "head in the sand" about all this. There were about thirty or forty styles but globally they had over 200 styles.'

Robert Wade Smith – businessman

* * *

Finally, Wade Smith decided to take matters into his own hands. In November, 1982, he quit his job, jumped into a van and drove to Germany where he loaded up on Adidas stock. He then found premises on Slater Street, Liverpool and with a nervous smile he opened up for business.

* * *

'The shop was 500 square feet. Out of the 250 styles we put on sale, 200 were Adidas and 30 were Nike. There were a few Puma and a few also-rans. We planned to sell 26,000 in the first year. We actually did that in the first seven weeks. We sold 110,000 that year. We quadrupled our budget first year. It was fairy tale stuff. It became a phenomenon. In our second year we did a quarter of a million. It was like winning the lottery. Now we've got something like 40,000 square feet. See sports shops in those days were run by ex-footballers and sportsmen who were good at their sport but not so good in business.'

Robert Wade Smith

* * *

The choice of sportswear by major personalities was another crucial element to the development of this movement. Whatever they wore automatically triggered a dedicated hunting down of that particular style.

* * *

'There was a Fila tracksuit that Bjorn Borg wore, the Fila BJ. Someone decided to wear that and suddenly you couldn't get them anywhere except this one shop in Fulham. It was a Hooray Henry shop and suddenly you had every little Casual in London running in there and robbing the shop. In the end they put an iron grille on the door, a lock and they wouldn't let you in.'

Terry Farley

'There was a famous shop outside of Sheffield United which sold Barbour jackets. They'd go out there and rob that. Then they'd go to that John Smedley warehouse in Matlock and rob that as well.'

Frank Cartledge

'Bjorn Borg was wearing Fila. McEnroe was wearing Sergio Tacchini, Connors was wearing Cerrutti 1881 and again the fans were bringing back Head bags full of expensive designer sports wear. That was between in 1980 and 1982 and we started to sell it in the shop in 1983. That was the Casual boom and that evolved into the Chevignon, Fiorucci and Chipie era. That was a mid-'80s thing and that went into Armani jeans in the late '80s and then Ralph Lauren in the early '90s, as well as Calvin Klein coming along in 1992. Then there's Paul Smith who was around in London in the '80s but in the provinces didn't mean anything until the '90s.'

Robert Wade Smith

* * *

In London, a major Casual shop was Moda on the Tower Bridge Road which sold T-shirts with Bermondsey, Moda emblazoned across them as well as Armani and Ricardo Beeny jackets. Another outlet was Stuarts on the Uxbridge Road.

Formerly a sportswear shop, the shop's manager Stuart had started changing his stock, adding other items such as Italian knitwear Gabicci and Farah trousers. Soon he was a clothes shop and in about 1978, a new breed started shopping there.

* * *

'They started stocking things like Pringle jumpers and Gabicci crewneck jumpers. So we started buying that stuff as well.'

Terry Farley

* * *

As his shop started to pick up speed, Stuart, the manager, described by many as a 'wheeler-dealer', sensed something was going on. So when one day he discovered that some of his regular customers were in a band, it

THE SOUL STYLISTS

didn't take too long for the dollar signs to start turning in his fevered imagination.

* * *

'We used to go to Stuart's in Shepherd's Bush along the Uxbridge Road and for a while the guy Stuart who ran it was our manager. We were in a band and we were wearing the gear so we thought put two and two together. We saw the parallel with the Mod thing.

'Unfortunately, it was picked up on by Garry Bushell at *Sounds* and I really am not sure if his heart is in the right place or not. We were sort of pop–rocky and I think that's why we never really hit it off as a Casual band because we were not a soul band.'

Mick Robinson

* * *

As the styles differed all over the country so too did musical tastes. In London, soul music was the preferred soundtrack. Later on, it became Acid House.

* * *

'You'd get stuff like Shannon's "Let The Music Play" and that kind of early electro stuff being played in all these local clubs. Like Maze were massive yet they were completely underground. They'd sell out Hammersmith Odeon for a week yet no one mainstream would have them. Later on Luther Vandross was quite popular. Everyone used to listen to the Philly stuff as well, the back catalogue.'

Mick Robinson

'In London, the Lyceum was where they used to go on a Saturday night and there were serious rucks in there. The music was pretty wanky soul music. There was nothing cutting-edge. The girls looked good though. They wore pleated skirts, silk blouses with these little tie things. I don't think they made a conscious effort to look cool it was just that if you saw five of them in a group they really stood out.'

Terry Farley

* * *

Out of London, the music changed dramatically although Sheffield and Liverpool seemed to share a similar taste for soul.

* * *

'In Sheffield – this was when people were wearing Pods, stretched jeans and mohair jumpers – there was this club called Pennies and it seemed to cross the gap between people who were Punks and others. It was the nearest you would get to a gay night and these lads were in there as well. The music was jazz-funk crossed with Northern Soul and things like Sheffield music from ABC and the Human League. Then there was the Limit which attracted a lot of Casuals and that was music from right across the board from the Jesus and Mary Chain and Bauhaus to contemporary R&B.'

Frank Cartledge

'The music was more of an unconscious thing. In Liverpool there was a club called Checkmates and it played very eclectic music and there was another one called the Swinging Apple and on an average night there you would hear Gina X mixed in with Barry White. I think what grew out of this period was a sense of defiance. As people went round the country and looked different they would be getting a lot of stick from people. The only thing I have ever seen taken up unanimously by everyone was first of all

The Jam and later on The Specials. UB40 were big as well which might have a lot to do with the pot-smoking culture.'

Kevin Sampson

* * *

These are the Soul Stylists, and amphetamines have always been a part of their armour. At first, Casuals necked speed and marijuana. Then Ecstasy and Acid House arrived and the whole world changed.

* * *

'I think the Casual thing died after that. People were still going to football but the cooler people who looked great at matches couldn't fight very well and then you had the people who fought very well but looked crap. The cool people filtered off into the club scene, the late rare-groove and then early Acid House thing. The football thing carried on with the violent people.'

Terry Farley

'I still used to go to football but not as much. I remember going to Chelsea one day. It must have been about early 1988 and Farley and all that lot were there but they'd become hippies overnight. They all had ponchos on and they were completely chilled out and non-aggressive. It was like a real jaw-dropping moment.'

Mick Robinson

'It wasn't a poncho. It was dungarees. I remember it because everyone laughed at me on the terraces. And a month later they were all wearing them. But you know what I really do long for is the moment when I walk down the street and see twenty eighteen-year-old kids who look fucking great. But I just don't see them. The trouble now is that people who are forty are wearing the same clothes as the kids. And until they find something so new and fresh it's going to carry on like this for a long time.

Terry Farley

'Shaun Ryder was famed for his haircut in the "Step On" video but that was a uniform haircut for Casuals at the time, the slick shiny centre-part bob. That whole culture (Acid House) affected all sorts of football mobs. I remember a lot of vivid colours, in particular the colour peach. You could never imagine yourself wearing white and orange but if it had the word Chevignon on it . . . Personally, I blame Acid House.'

Kevin Sampson

'Dolce and Gabbana came in the mid-'90s and then obviously in the late '90s Prada sports, Gucci, Helmut Lang. It is getting more sophisticated. The core customer who were in their mid- to late-teens in the '70s and who are now in their mid-'30s, might buy fewer items but they're still buying top-end. More subtle as well, they don't want anything with a label on it. For three years now the branding has got more subtle. Prada now is just a red stripe on the sleeve. It doesn't say Prada on it. The same for Helmut Lang and Paul Smith.'

Robert Wade Smith

Epilogue

ONE SUMMER'S DAY IN 1989 I was out shopping for Wallabees. I'd been told there was a shop down King's Road that sold them. Evidently, half of London had also heard months before me. The queue stretched down the road and inside the shop was a shoe frenzy – a whole new generation of Modernists were getting theirs. You could see there was a new look emerging.

I left the shop and further down the road a kid on a day-glo (Acid House) style Vespa went by. Around that time I'd shop a lot in Duffer of St George's. Just up from it was Black Market Records – proper packed on a Saturday morning with kids buying the latest American imports, the new beats spilling out of the speakers and onto D'Arblay Street. And I felt a kind of reassurance that the beat truly does go on. The clothes change, the drugs too, and the music moves on but the attitude remains unchanged. Which is why we leave this book open ended.

Paul Weller

The secret is still locked up.

Robert Hall

THE SOUL STYLISTS WERE:

Eddie Harvey – still writes and performs and also lectures in music

John Simon – runs J. Simon in London's Covent Garden

Val Wilmer is a distinguished writer whose books include *As Serious As Your Life* and *Mama Said There Would Be Days Like This*

Carol Tulloch is currently working on a book about black fashion

Lloyd Bradley is a writer and the author of *(Bass Culture) When Reggae Was King*

Carlo Manzi runs Carlo Manzi Rentals, a male costume hire business

Eugene Manzi is an independent publicist and lifelong Mod

Gary Herman is the author of a book on The Who and now works in computers

Patrick Uden is the head of Uden Associates, a major independent TV company

David Cole is the editor of *In The Basement*, a top notch soul fanzine

Chris Hill is still a massive Georgie Fame fan and successful DJ

Phil Smee is a successful designer

Robert Hall is a marketing director

Ian R. Hebditch is a lecturer and still adores The Action

Ann Sullivan is an original Mod

So is Eileen Barnes

Liz Woodcroft is a barrister and author of *Goodbadwoman*

Gary Kingham – works for William Hunt and is a lifelong Stylist

Jesse Hector is a musician and still has a great haircut

Terry Wheeler works in the rag trade and smiles a lot

Ady Croasdell compiles great soul collections and also runs the 6T's
club in London, considered by many to be the best soul club in the
country

Nigel Mann lives in Leicester and was an original Skinhead

Jim Cox lives in London and still wears great sheepskin coats

George Georgiou runs a successful design business called General
Practice

James Ferguson works as an illustrator for the *Financial Times*. His work
can be seen in Nick Knight's *Skinhead* book.

Terry Farley helped start the influential Boys Own label and is a
major DJ

Stuart Malloy is the head of Jones in London's Covent Garden

Dave Clegg lives in Nottingham where he fills his head with the sweetest
soul

Brian Taylor lives in Bradford where he keeps his 1965 white Ben
Sherman in pristine condition.

Ian Dewhurst DJed at Wigan Casino and now runs Simply Vinyl

Gilly and Tats discovered the singer Little Ann and are fully dedicated
members to the soul cause

Dave Prest supports Bradford FC and great soul records

Norman Jay has proved to be one of the most influential DJs on
London's club scene. His compilation *Good Times* has just been
released on Nuphonic Records

Paul McKee is the video commissioner at One Little Indian Records

Ean Carter still dances to 'Always There'

Steven Harris is the author of *Dear Alan, Dear Harry*

Mick Mahoney is a playwright of great repute

Kevin Sampson is an author of great repute

Frank Cartledge is a major lecturer

Robert Wade Smith runs his own business in Liverpool

Mick Robinson runs the successful Pavilion Hotel in Brighton
Richard Simpson is a clothes stylist

There are three others I would also like to note for their great support
and help. They are Dean Cavanagh, Dan Sharp and Kevin Rowland.

A SOUL STYLIST RECORD SELECTION

'Things To Come' by Dizzy Gillespie

'Blue Serge', 'Rock Skippin' and 'Ummg' by Duke Ellington and Billy Strayhorn

'Manteca', 'Cubana Be' and 'Stay On It' by the Dizzy Gillespie Big Band

'Our Delight', 'Dameronia' and 'Sid's Delight' by Tad Dameron

'Cool Blues', 'Confirmation' and 'Okedokey' (with Machito) by Charlie Parker

'Godchild', 'Israel', and 'Jeru' by the Miles Davis None

'Walkin' Shoes' and 'Line for Lyons' by the Gerry Mulligan Quartet

'Sweet Lorraine' by Nat King Cole

'Just A Gigolo' by the Joe Mooney Quartet

'Move' and 'Lightly Politely' by the Johnny Dankworth Seven

SELECTED BY EDDIE HARVEY

'Sack O' Woe' by Cannonball Adderley

'Parchman Farm' by Mose Allison

'Whirlybird' by Count Basie

'Blue Monk' by Art Blakey and Thelonious Monk

'The Right Time' by Ray Charles with Margie Hendrix and the Raelettes

'Yeh Yeh' by Georgie Fame

'Doin' Alright' by Dexter Gordon

'Blues Backstage' by Lambert Hindricks and Ross

'Long Distance Call' by Muddy Waters

'Big Fine Gal' by Jimmy Witherspoon (Vogue 78 r.p.m. version)

SELECTED BY VAL WILMER

'Baby Don't You Do It' by Marvin Gaye

'She Blew A Good Thing' by The Poets

'Meeting Over Yonder' by The Impressions

'The Real Thing' by Tina Britt

'Mine Exclusively' by The Olympics

'Take Me In Your Arms' by Kim Weston

'I'm Gonna Miss You' by The Artistics

'See Saw' by Don Covay and the Goodtimers

'Open The Door To Your Heart' by Daryl Banks

'Better Use Your Head' by Little Anthony and the Imperials

SELECTED BY IAN R. HEBDITCH

'Live Injection' by The Upsetters

'Sufferer' by The Kingstonians

'Jackpot' by The Pioneers

'Reggae Hit The Town' by The Ethiopians

'Too Proud To Beg' by The Uniques

'The Cooler' by The Wrigglers

'Nana' by The Slickers

'I Love You' by Derrick Morgan

'Baby Why' by The Cables

'Hold Down' by The Kingstonians

SELECTED BY JIM COX

THE SOUL STYLISTS

'Helpless' by Kim Weston

'I'll Never Stop Loving You' by Carla Thomas

'She Blew A Good Thing' by The Poets

'You're Gonna Make Me Love You' by Sandi Sheldon

'Getting To Me' by Ben E. King

'You Turned My Bitter Into Sweet' by Mary Love

'I Have Faith In You' by Edwin Starr

'Hand It Over' by Chuck Jackson

'Love Runs Out' by Willie Hutch

'Perfect Love' by The Diplomats

SELECTED BY ADY CROASDELL

'Sweet Power Your Embrace' by James Mason

'Always There' by Side Effect

'Runaway' by Loleatta Holloway

'See You When I Get There' by Lou Rawls

'Ten Percent' by Double Exposure

'Inside America' by Juggy Murray Jones

'Los Conquistadores Chocolates' by Johnny Hammond

'Salsa Mama' by Doug Richardson

'Body Contact Contract' by The Trammps

'Got To Get Your Own' by Reuben Wilson

SELECTED BY NORMAN JAY

'Expansions' by Lonnie Liston Smith

'The Bottle' by Joe Bataan

'Get Loose' by Aleem

'Ain't No Sunshine' by Sivuca

'(How We Gonna Make) The Black Nation Rise' by Brother D. and the
    Collective Effort

'Catch The Beat' by T. Ski Valley

'Candidate For Love' by T. S. Monk

THE SOUL STYLISTS

'The Sound of Music' by Daytona

'Do Fries Go With That Shake' by George Clinton

'Encore' by Cheryl Lynn

SELECTED BY TERRY FARLEY

BIBLIOGRAPHY

Mama Said There Would Be Days Like This by Val Wilmer

Gentleman by Bernard Roetzel

The Hip by Roy Carr, Brian Case and Fred Dellar

Reggae the Rough Guide by Steve Barrow and Peter Dalton

The In Crowd by Mike Ritson and Stuart Russell

Soho in the Fifties by Daniel Farson

Jazz Man: The amazing story of Ronnie Scott by John Fordham

London Live by Tony Bacon

The Skinhead Bible by George Marshall

Folk Devils and Moral Panics by Stanley Cohen

Tongs Ya Bass by R.G. MacCallum

Windrush by Mike and Trevor Phillips

The Sharper Word: A Mod Anthology by Paolo Hewitt

Soulsville USA by Rob Bowman

Sweet Soul Music by Peter Guralnick

Alexis Korner by Harry Shapiro

The Nick Tosches Reader by Nick Tosches

THE SOUL STYLISTS